TRUE LIGHTS

True Lights

Talks on Saints and Leaders of the Christian Church

BY

J. W. C. WAND, D.D.

Treasurer of St. Paul's; formerly Bishop of London

LONDON

A. R. MOWBRAY & Co. Limited

NEW YORK: MOREHOUSE-GORHAM CO.

© *A. R. Mowbray & Co. Limited 1958*

First published in 1958

PRINTED IN GREAT BRITAIN BY
A. R. MOWBRAY & CO. LIMITED IN THE CITY OF OXFORD
7760

PREFACE

WHEN I was an incumbent and could arrange services to my own satisfaction, I used to mark holy days by reading extracts at evensong from a well-known book on the saints. The elderly ladies who attended the daily office professed themselves much edified. For my own part I was glad to find my knowledge of the great heroes of the faith refreshed and widened.

Since then it has often been my lot to give broadcast talks on the saints. Consequently when I was invited to produce a volume of sermons for publication, it seemed possible that a collection of such talks might be useful not only for private reading, but also for helping over-burdened incumbents to infuse a little extra variety into weekday services.

Such a volume may also be specially appropriate at a time when the Church is considering how far it may be advisable to include post-Reformation worthies in the kalendar. It must surely be good for us to remind ourselves that genuine sainthood did not cease in the sixteenth century. The 'cloud of witnesses' continues and increases from generation to generation. In the last four hundred years the Anglican Communion has added its own distinguished members to the brotherhood. It is good that we should remember ancient and modern together, even as we recall with gratitude that 'they without us will not be made perfect.'

✠ WM: WAND.

For they the Church's princes are,
Triumphant leaders in the war,
In heavenly courts a warrior band,
True lights to lighten every land.

J. M. NEALE
Hymns A. & M. 430

CONTENTS

TRUE LIGHTS

INTRODUCTION

WHAT IS A SAINT?

A SAINT is not, of course, a person who has always been holy, in the sense that he has exhibited nothing but virtue from the time of his birth. In *The Shepherd of Hermas*, a book which nearly found a place in the New Testament, you will find a curious phrase 'To the Saints who have sinned,' and if you will turn to the Epistles of the New Testament itself you will find even St. Paul exhorting the saints not to commit quite elementary sins, such as stealing and lying.

The fact is that the term 'saint' was originally applied to all Christians, because they were people who had been 'sainted,' that is to say, dedicated to God in baptism. Gradually, however, the term began to have a special reference to the heroes of the Christian life.

It is probable that the first step in the recognition of such heroes was taken during those early centuries when the Church suffered persecution at the hands of the Roman Emperors. Yearly commemorations were held at the tombs of the martyrs, and sometimes the slab beneath which a famous Christian was buried would form the altar at which the commemorative Eucharist was celebrated. The anniversary of his death came to be called the 'birthday' of the martyr, the day on which he was born into the fullness of eternal life. Another practice which extended this popular recognition of the saints and which dates from at least the middle of the third century was that of giving the name of a saint to a child who happened to be born on his commemoration day.

This recognition not only of a saint, but also of his particular festival, was the beginning from which developed the whole kalendar of the saints. At first, each local community would have its own list of such heroes. Gradually, as the Church grew stronger and communication between the different local communities became more completely stabilized, these lists would be shared and combined until they became sufficiently comprehensive to serve the Church as a whole. Our own English scholar saint of the seventh century, the Venerable Bede, seems to have been the first to issue a completely comprehensive list of the 'saints,' giving biographical details of those whom the Church regularly commemorated.

The saints, then, are the people whose names are inscribed on the Church's Roll of Honour. We may now go on to ask what entitled them to such honour. How were they distinguished from their fellows? They revealed two main characteristics which are common to all of them alike. The first was an intense belief in the reality of God; and the second an equally intense confidence in the possibility of goodness.

With regard to the first. They possessed that firm grasp of the reality of God which made the unseen world far more real to them than the world of material things. The spiritual realities were actually more important to them than the food they ate, the clothes they wore, the money they earned. They possessed the power of pulling aside the veil of material existence and looking into the unseen where abide the eternal verities. So they learnt to 'look not upon the things that are seen, but upon the things that are not seen, for the things that are seen are temporal; the things that are not seen are eternal.' Thus the saint, whether he was a lover of nature, like St. Francis, who could preach to the birds, or whether he was impervious to the appeal of nature, like St. Bernard who could walk all day long by the beautiful Lake of Geneva and never even see it, was attuned to the very core of existence and could hear the heart of the world beating below all physical appearance. His was the special capacity for seeing God,

> The gift that sees with glance profound
> The secret soul of things,
> And in the silence hears the sound
> Of vast and viewless wings!

For most of us such a gift is so strange as to seem almost incredible. We are immersed in appearances, so taken up with superficialities that it is only by the greatest effort that we can remind ourselves of the unseen world at all. But the Saints got back to that storied condition of the newly-created soul where it was possible to move continually in the presence of God, and where in the sunset cool of the garden God walked and talked habitually with man.

It has been said that 'in these incredulous and superficial days Christianity understood at such a depth appears a prodigious originality.' These men and women made the old common truth shine again with its first uncommon lustre, and in them it came to life again.

The prime characteristic of the Saints is this intense belief in the reality of God. The other special characteristic is their firm conviction of the possibility of goodness. They believe without any doubt that the attainment of virtue is no mere chimera of hysterical imagination but is a sober duty for the child of God.

An interesting French writer has suggested that the essential *differentia* of the saints is their capacity to hate evil. 'The execration of evil,' he says, 'is the rarest of virtues and the most forgotten of glories.' I should have said myself that their distinctive character lies not so much in their negative hatred of evil as in their positive passion for goodness. They are chiefly characterized by the intense fervour of that passion. It is not an ordinary inclination to be good. They show a noble scorn for mediocrity, and their sanctity is the very antithesis of lukewarmness. The genius always feels more intensely than other men, and they are the geniuses of the moral life. They love good more passionately, and hate evil more fiercely, than their fellows. Their prayer is 'without ceasing.' Their love is 'fervent.' Their work is 'zealous.' They show just that extra quality which is the difference between the average Christian attainment and complete devotion.

> Oh, the little more, and how much it is!
> And the little less, and what worlds away!

Genius is sometimes said to be an infinite capacity for taking pains. So saintliness is an infinite capacity for showing usual virtues in an unusual degree.

If those two gifts, namely an intense belief in the reality of God and confidence in the possibility of goodness, are the basic characteristics of all the saints alike, we must not suppose that all saints are made in the same mould. On the contrary, they display an infinite variety. Each age, for instance, produces its own characteristic expression of saintliness. But what proves admirable in one age actually may be distasteful to another. Some modern people find the old Desert Saints positively repellent. And, indeed, it is easy for us to make a mock of a person like St. Simon Stylites, who rested for so long aloft upon his pillar that he seemed more animal than human. Yet the historian, trying to put himself back into the temper of the times, will tell us that this man influenced many for righteousness. From his pillar he was able through his almost savage austerities to convert hundreds of the semi-barbarian people who crowded to see and to hear him.

On the other hand St. Francis of Assisi, who was not a particularly popular figure in his own day, appeals to many moderns as perhaps the greatest and most Christ-like of the Saints; and many who would never dream of imitating his extreme poverty are nevertheless quite ready to rhapsodize over his love of nature and his devotion to animals.

Again, in a time of war we are very ready to appreciate the military and patriotic qualities of Joan of Arc, although she, too, was in advance of the contemporary leaders of her nation. They betrayed her to a cruel death and she waited five centuries for canonization. Yet it was veneration for her that did more than anything else to keep the French nation together at a critical period of the First World War.

So varied are the forms of goodness that the Saints are representative of every class in the community and of almost every type of character. High and low, rich and poor, learned and unlearned, mystics and men of affairs—all alike are represented on the roll of those who have shewn this supreme confidence in God and goodness.

It is not to be thought, however, that their attainment of this pre-eminence was a simple or an easy thing. They were the great Christian athletes, and like all athletes they had to go through their period of special training. Indeed, it may be said that life for them was one long

B

struggle, although they were happier in that struggle than they could have been in any other condition.

We are sometimes inclined to forget the essential asceticism which was the characteristic of the life of all the Saints. This indeed, especially in the case of the hermits, sometimes implied terrible austerities. It is interesting to notice that monasteries were to some extent a protest against such exaggerations. Men and women who wished to live on a specially high level of Christianity, on a level that seemed to many to be that of essential Christianity, were gathered into communities so that their life could be regulated by authority and they should not compete with one another in the maltreatment of their own bodies.

But whether in the monasteries or outside it was always recognized that if a man wished to pursue the ends of the spirit he must be very careful to subdue the flesh. The modern theory that you must let the flesh go its own way and do nothing to restrain its desires is a complete contradiction of the view held universally by the saints. They might have agreed that to give way to the flesh is 'natural.' But they would have said that man is not expected to be merely natural: he has been redeemed and given a supernatural capacity. Their conception of man was just as much higher than the naturalistic conception as man himself is higher than the brute beasts. For that reason they felt that if man wanted to attain to his operative possibilities he must hold himself under a severe discipline.

These saints and leaders were not all members of clerical or monastic Orders. Many of them lived an everyday life in the world. The particular scope of their asceticism differed from individual to individual. Many of them would not be recognized as ascetics at all by the ordinary man, because as far as could be seen their life differed in no superficial respect from that of their neighbours. But there was one essential element of asceticism that did characterize them all, and that was a complete interior surrender of all that they were and all that they possessed to God. Not one of them considered that the things he possessed were his own or intended merely for his own enjoyment. All believed that they belonged to God; they surrendered everything to Him; and they were perfectly ready to enjoy only just so much of worldly pleasures as God handed back to them.

And that brings me to the last point I want to make, which is this—that the lives of the Saints should be a great incentive to us in our struggles. They are the great Cloud of Witnesses who surround us while we carry on the contest in the arena where they have already struggled so nobly. The fact that they have done well shews us what can be done and gives us confidence and courage.

Dean Inge used to say that if he were ever tempted to give up his belief in the Christian faith, the recollection of the Saints would always enable him to recover his confidence. Certainly we all admire a good man. However we may be divided in theology or politics we are at least united in our respect for uncommon goodness. The lives of the Saints remind us that that which we so admire in others is possible for ourselves.

Napoleon said that every soldier carries a Field Marshal's baton in his haversack. So every Christian has set before him the possibility of becoming a saint. As baptized Christians we already possess the potentiality of sainthood. It is for us to live 'as becometh saints.' The recollection of the great heroes of the Christian faith should give us the incentive to this endeavour. They already are beyond anxiety. They have fought the good fight and have won their victory. The white robes, the palms, the crowns, in which the biblical imagery clothes them, are the shining symbols of a triumphant joy that transcends the capacities of mortal language to describe and ensures a peace that passes all present understanding. God grant that as we too share in their warfare we may share also in their victory.

> They were mortal, too, like us;
>   O, when we like them must die,
> May our souls translated thus
>   Triumph, reign, and shine on high.

1

ST. CLEMENT, THE SCHOLAR

I WISH to begin our talks on Saints and Leaders by telling you something about the first of the great Christian scholars. He is the teacher who is known to us as Clement of Alexandria.

There are a number of other Clements in Early Church history, but this one is known as Clement of Alexandria because it was in that city that his great work was done.

He was not an Alexandrian by birth. It is probable that he was born in another great University town, that of Athens. The date of his birth must have been somewhere about A.D. 150. In all probability his father was a freedman, and certainly both his parents were pagans.

Clement himself was brought up as a pagan. But even in his early life he evidently took religion seriously, because it is generally agreed that he was initiated into the mysteries of Eleusis, the most famous of the pagan cults of the period. We shall see presently how this initiation so impressed itself upon him that it affected his whole method of teaching Christianity in later days.

He went through his university course at Athens, and although Christianity did not for a very long time really conquer this greatest of all the cities of ancient learning, it was while he was here that Clement himself was converted.

It is interesting that we know nothing of the precise manner of that conversion. It may seem paradoxical to call such lack of knowledge 'interesting'; but when you come to think of it, it is really extraordinarily instructive. Nearly all the great teachers of Christianity have left us some account of their conversion, because it represented a violent break with their old life. But Clement never talks of such a cataclysm.

The reason is that his progress from paganism to Christianity was by way of a gradual enlightenment. It was typical of the scholar's search after truth. Here was no brand suddenly plucked from the burning, no despairing soul suddenly lifted out of the morass of sin, no protagonist suddenly changed from a persecutor to one of the persecuted. In other words here is no Paul, or Augustine, or Luther, or even Wesley; but one to whom the truth came like the light of dawn that shines more and more unto the perfect day.

After his conversion Clement set out on his travels. Students of the day did not content themselves with study at one university, but if they had the means they journeyed all over the civilized world to sit at the feet of one famous teacher after another. Clement carried this custom into the life of the Christian. He went to the greatest cities around the Mediterranean, seeking the most outstanding masters of Christianity.

It was thus that he came ultimately to Alexandria. Here a Christian school had been established under the shadow of the University. Its teacher at this time was Pantaenus; but he must have been obliged to work in comparative secrecy because, although Clement came for the express purpose of meeting him, it was only with considerable difficulty that he could find him.

The object of the school was chiefly to instruct inquiring pagans. It was, of course, not officially connected with the University. Nor was it closely attached to the Church, for at this time it was largely free from episcopal control.

But it became one of the most important institutions in the whole of the ancient Christian world.

Alexandria was the university where the most advanced learning of the Greeks was brought into close contact with the best Jewish teaching. It was there that the great Jewish scholar, Philo, had endeavoured to make the Laws of Moses square with Platonic philosophy. This conjuncture of Greek and Jew had already produced the Septuagint, the famous Greek translation of the Old Testament. It was a matter of great importance that Christianity should have its representative scholarly institution just at this point where Jewish and Greek learning had been combined.

In the old days it had been possible to say that not many men of learning had accepted Christianity. But now at least there was an opportunity for Christianity to claim a place for itself in the learned world; and it was under Clement that the new departure achieved a marked success.

For ten years Clement taught in company with Pantaenus, and it says much for the character of both men that although Clement's fame soon surpassed that of his master, there is no sign of quarrel or jealousy between them. Then on the death of Pantaenus Clement himself became the recognized head of the school.

This position he held for about twelve years. In 202, however, the Roman Government made an attempt to stop conversions to Christianity. This, of course, involved a special attack upon the schools and colleges which were responsible for such conversions.

Clement had to make up his mind whether he would stay and forfeit his life, or whether he would take refuge in flight. Opinion among Christians was much divided as to which was the correct course to pursue. Some

challenged recognition, and actually demanded martyrdom; others remembered the Gospel injunction, 'When
they persecute you in one city, flee to another.' This
latter was the course actually adopted by Clement,
and for some further years he wandered about in various
cities.

We hear of him once again about nine years later,
when one of his old pupils, who had now become a
bishop, writes of him in a letter to the Church of Antioch.
He seems to have frequented the towns where he could
find good libraries and where he could carry on his
writing. He was apparently well-to-do. During his stay
in Alexandria he had been ordained to the priesthood,
so that he would be sure of a warm welcome and hos-
pitality wherever he went. A few more years passed
by and another letter from the same episcopal pupil
refers to Clement as having 'gone before.' This is the
only information we have of his death.

The real interest of Clement's life lies not in the record
of his activities, but in his writings. He was a true
scholar, with no particle of the fanatic or controversialist
in his composition. He had no aim but to discover and
impart the truth. He believed that as all truth comes
from God, so every particle of truth if followed to its
conclusion must lead back to God, and he could think
of no more noble occupation than to be concerned in
this continuous search for knowledge.

It is probable indeed that, like another early Christian
scholar, he wore the recognized garb of the philosopher,
and he certainly did everything he could to present
Christianity in the light of the supreme philosophy.
In fact, he used as descriptive of his religion a word which
was at this time commonly used only by the opponents
of orthodox Christianity. It was the word Gnosis, or

knowledge, implying a secret or esoteric truth, something which was reserved for the initiates and hidden from the vulgar. But Clement would not allow either the word or the thing to be monopolized by any organization outside the Church.

Clement claimed that the religion of the Church was the true Gnosis, and he said that his object was to lead his pupils to become true Gnostics. In much the same way a Christian teacher to-day might seek to wrest their self-chosen title from the Humanists and claim that the only true Humanism was to be found in Christianity. Clement's was no narrow mind, and he believed that adumbrations of the truth, shadowy reflections of it, could be found almost everywhere. 'The true scribe,' he says, 'brings all kinds of learning into the Gospel net.' His favourite theme is that the world was prepared for the coming of Christianity by Greek philosophy as much as by Judaism. He was even bolder in the way in which he set out his system. He actually built up his Christian teaching on the lines of the successive stages of initiation into the pagan mysteries, that is Preparation, Initiation, Revelation.

He considered that for the ignorant merely to believe and obey might be enough; but for the intelligent it was necessary to use the reason. He realized, of course, that there were difficulties in the way of an intelligent faith even within the pages of Scripture. How, for instance, could one explain many of the crude and unpleasant things in the Old Testament? There were those who felt the difficulty so strongly that they would have liked to cut away the Old Testament altogether. Nowadays, of course, we explain them by our evolutionary theory, and endeavour to show that in the infancy of the race

God had to speak with stammering lips to His children in order that He might be understood by them.

Clement adopted neither of these expedients. What he did was to use the allegorical method of interpretation, explaining the more obvious crudities as not to be taken literally but as symbols of higher spiritual truth. This allegorical method became a fixed characteristic of the Alexandrian school, and made it possible for people to use the Old Testament with edification all through the Middle Ages until such time as our modern and more scientific methods came into vogue.

I must not spend too long talking about Clement's theology, although I am very anxious that you should admire this quiet scholar trying to win the learned world of his day for Christ. But there is one signal service performed by him for our own day which I must not fail to mention. Some of you are old enough to remember the difficulty that was caused for Christianity when the theory of evolution first burst upon the religious world. Indeed you know that some Christians have not been able to assimilate it even yet.

Well, for English-speaking Christians the victory was won by a group of scholars and theologians at Oxford, the famous authors of a book known as *Lux Mundi*, which was first published in 1889. What is extremely interesting to us at the moment is that those men found the means of reconciling a belief in Christianity with an acceptance of the theory of evolution in the teaching of Clement and his friends. It would be hardly too much to say that but for Clement of Alexandria *Lux Mundi* could never have been written.

And now, in conclusion, I want to give you an example of Clement's style. This is not taken from any of his more learned works, but from a simple sermon on the subject of The Rich Young Man. It is a story, and it is an especially interesting story because it illustrates the love and the courage of no less a person than the Apostle John. It relates an incident in the life of St. John when, after the death of the tyrant Domitian, he had been released from his exile on the island of Patmos and had undertaken the oversight of the churches in Ephesus and the surrounding district.

He had committed a promising young man to the care of a local bishop, only to find on his return that the man had disappeared into the wild and become the leader of a band of robbers. 'Just as he was,' says Clement, 'he rode straight away from the church itself; and coming to the place, he is seized by the outpost of the robbers; he neither flees, nor asks to be freed, but shouts, "For this purpose am I come; take me away to your leader." The leader, armed as he was, waited for a while; but, when he recognized John on his approach, he was ashamed and turned to flight. But the Apostle, forgetful of his own age, pursued him with all his might, crying out, "Why dost thou fly from me, my child, thine own father, unarmed and old? Pity me, my child, fear not; thou hast yet hope of life; I will be surety to Christ for thee; if it be needful, I will willingly suffer the death thou deservest, as the Lord suffered death for us; on thy behalf will I give my own life. Stand, believe, Christ has sent me."' Needless to say the young man could not resist such an entreaty, but dissolved in tears and was restored, after prolonged penance, to the Church.

That is the story, and having heard it I think you will understand why F. D. Maurice described Clement, who preserved it for us, as 'that one of the old fathers whom we should all have reverenced most as a teacher, and loved best as a friend.'

2

ORIGEN, THE PATHFINDER

THERE is no more illustrious name among the scholars of the Early Church than that of Origen, yet he is not a saint in the strict sense, as he was never actually canonized. I should myself describe him as a Pathfinder, and the extent of his genius may be judged from the fact that we are still trying to answer some of the questions he raised. As he was much more than a scholar I will give you three scenes from his life before speaking about the academic side of his work.

The curtain goes up on the drama at the beginning of the third century, when the Emperor Septimus Severus was trying to destroy the Christian Church. The special point of his attack was the system by which the Christians gained recruits, and his hand fell heavily upon the School at Alexandria, where, as we have seen, on the fringe of the greatest University of the ancient world, the Church had established a kind of college to influence the undergraduates and men of learning.

The Head of the School, the fine scholar and gentleman, Clement, was a marked man and he was compelled to flee. Looking round for a new Head to succeed him, the bishop could think of no one better than his brightest pupil, the seventeen-year-old Origen.

Origen knew something about persecution already. His own father had suffered martyrdom, and it is a mystery how Origen himself escaped. On one occasion indeed he was only prevented from rushing into danger by the fact that his mother had hidden his clothes; and perhaps it was her watchfulness, as well as his own youth, which saved him. But there he is, at the age of seventeen the head of a famous college, and bearing upon his youthful shoulders the responsibility not only for the management of the school, but also for the support of his widowed mother and her family.

The second scene is of Origen at the full height of his teaching powers. At first his influence was mainly exercised through his lectures. He was a true scholar, an omnivorous reader, who felt that he could not pursue his own subject properly without making himself familiar with the best and widest teaching of the day. He had at one time possessed a useful library of secular literature, but he had been compelled to sell these valuable books in order to provide a pittance for the family he had to support. Then, through laborious years of teaching, he had to subsist as best he could.

But a great change came when, through the kindness of a wealthy convert, he was provided with no fewer than six shorthand writers and six copyists. He was now able to exercise an even greater influence through his books than through his oral lectures. His industry was prodigious, and his output almost incredible. One of the early historians credits him with no fewer than six thousand books, and although that may have been an exaggeration, we know that many hundreds were collected in one library at Caesarea, where later the Latin scholar Jerome was to find them of the greatest value in his own biblical studies.

All the time he was teaching and writing Origen was also learning. Like his teacher Clement, he was no narrow ecclesiastic, accepting views on authority without examining them from every point of view. He attended the lectures of the greatest pagan philosopher of the day, and studied carefully the work of the most able champion of paganism against Christianity. The result was that he himself attracted many of the greatest scholars of the period. He influenced them not only by his learning, but also by his generous enthusiasm for all that was best and highest in contemporary ideals.

That enthusiasm sometimes led him to a pitch of self-sacrifice which he was afterwards to regret. Although at this time he escaped martyrdom he subjected himself to an act of self-mutilation in a too literal interpretation of our Lord's words about those who make themselves eunuchs for the kingdom of heaven's sake. This act caused a great deal of trouble, especially when one of his friends among the bishops ordained him to the priesthood and his own bishop and many of his colleagues in Alexandria disputed the validity of the ordination.

Difficulties grew so great that finally he had to leave Alexandria, and in the final scene we find him at Caesarea, surrounded by friends and disciples and still piling up the magnificent total of volumes that were to fill the library there. It was now the middle of the third century and once again persecution broke out. The Emperor Decius did not, like his predecessor Severus, attack only one section of the Christian organization, but he made a systematic effort to find every joint in the Church's armour. Origen was marked down for special attention. The government's purpose was to make him prove false to his Christian vows. Consequently he was not slain outright, but put through a round of torture in the hope of making him apostatize. He was still alive when the persecution ended, but he never completely recovered from his sufferings. He lingered on for two years and then died in A.D. 254.

Those three scenes give you some idea of the life of this great scholar and will enable you to picture his external circumstances for yourselves. I must now try to say something about his teaching, and so enable you to realize how the epithet Pathfinder as applied to him can be justified. I will try to give you three different aspects of his work. We will listen as he dictates to his secretaries and hear what kind of thing he had to talk about.

First, he was most interested in the Bible. He was interested in it both from the devotional point of view and also from the point of view of the scholar. He was the first to recognize that if you are to explain the Bible properly you must begin by making sure that you have a correct text. That is to say, you must know exactly what the original writers actually put down in their manuscripts. And then, because the Bible has been translated from one language into another, you must be quite sure that the translation is correct and that you have in the new language precisely what was said in the old.

In order to make sure of this double basis of all biblical study Origen caused to be compiled one of the most elaborate works ever composed. It was called the *Hexapla*: that is to say the Six-fold Book. It was so called because for the most part it consisted of six parallel columns. In these columns were given first the Hebrew of the Old Testament, and then the Hebrew put into Greek letters, and then, side by side, various translations into Greek.

In order to equip himself for this study, Origen had actually gone to the trouble of learning Hebrew. I don't know that he ever mastered it very fully, and failure to do so might account for the fact that he did not think very highly of the Hebrew text. Indeed, one of the reasons why he compiled the *Hexapla* was to persuade the Greek people that their principal version, known as the Septuagint, was every bit as good as the original Hebrew. It was much as if we told theological students to-day that they need not bother to learn Greek or Hebrew because the English version is better than either.

Curiously enough Origen's mistaken view about the small value of the Hebrew text was shared two centuries afterwards by St. Augustine. It was Jerome who used Origen's work to a better effect, and Jerome and Augustine very nearly quarrelled over the question. However, the fact remains that even if Origen made a mistake, his methods were the right ones, and he started biblical studies along the line of development from which we are only beginning to derive the greatest benefit in our own day.

But Origen was not satisfied with determining exactly what the Biblical writers said. Having once settled that important question, the next thing to do was to decide what they meant. Origen wrote volumes with this end in view on practically every book of the Bible. Some were sermons on isolated texts. Some were scholarly notes on biblical passages, and some were full commentaries on various books.

But here again Origen was not satisfied when he had determined precisely what the writers meant. He believed that the Bible was compiled to help people upon their road to heaven. And because he realized that some passages of the Bible in their superficial meaning are not altogether edifying, he laid it down that there were actually three different senses to be found in scripture. He compared the three with the body, the soul, and the spirit in man. The body was the literal, historical and grammatical meaning of the text. The soul was the moral lesson that could be derived from it. The spirit was the allegorical or mystical meaning which could lift a text from the ordinary plane of time and space into the region of eternal verity.

Of course this last is a very dangerous method of interpretation; but it was one which was extremely valuable because it helped to bridge the long gap before the science of historical criticism was developed. It was indeed the only way by which people could derive spiritual edification from considerable portions of the Old Testament all the way through the Middle Ages, and it survived long beyond the period of the Reformation. You can see a good example of it if you look at our Authorized Version of the Canticles, or Song of Songs. We know now that those songs were originally quite simply love songs, referring to the relations between a lover and his lass. But if you read the chapter headings in the Authorized Version you will see that they are explained as describing the relations between Christ and His Church. It was by such means that Origen found a way for people to understand and appreciate what he held to be the deeper meaning of the Word of God.

The next aspect of Origen's teaching, which is important, is his effort to work out a coherent system of knowledge and belief. As in the case of every true philosopher, it was abhorrent to him that any truth should not be fitted into the total explanation he conceived of the universe. He tried to combine together both the result of his rational thought as a philosopher and also the revelation that as a theologian he believed the Church had received from God. And here is the outline of his final explanation.

There has always been God. But as God is all-powerful there must always have been something upon which His power could be exercised. And that something is to be

C

found in the created universe: not the universe as we see it to-day, but a universe of spirits, all free and all equal. The means by which that universe was created was the Logos, or Word of God. He was not created, but He was eternally generated or born of God. Of the created spirits some exercised their freedom of will aright and became what we know as angels. Others went to the opposite extreme, chose nothing but evil, and became what we know as demons. But the remainder, who chose mingled evil and good became what we know as human beings. Our material world was created as a school or training ground for human spirits that they might find their way back to the felicity from which they had started. In order to enable them to find that way back, the Son of God united Himself with a human spirit, became Incarnate, and lived as one of themselves. While He instructed them both by precept and example, the Spirit of God worked in them to sanctify them or make them holy. This redemptive work was carried a step further in the death of Jesus upon the Cross by which the Word of God paid a ransom price to the Devil and so set men free from his clutches.

Origen looked forward to a final period when this time-process would be finished and all things would be restored to a state of perfection. He believed that in that perfection not only angels and human begins would share, but also the demons and even the Devil himself. They would live after the Resurrection in a state of perfection in which they would be clothed upon, certainly with bodies, but with spiritual bodies, not the material bodies that we wear to-day.

You will no doubt recognize at once how this view of Origen's compares with the Christian system that is commonly held among ourselves. In some respects, as for instance in his view of the eternal generation of the Son of God, Origen determined the set of Christian opinion for all time. But in other respects he has not carried the full weight of Christian opinion with him. Some centuries after his death people became very worried about his view of the resurrection body, and others began to ask, If all men in the end were to be saved, what was the special value in being a Christian? For these and similar doubts he was condemned as a heretic. Actually he was very far removed from the temper of the typical heretic. He closes the magnificent book in which he tries to work out this system with a sentiment revealing at once the greatest common sense and humility. 'Those are the ideas,' he says, 'which have presented themselves to me in thinking about the nature of God and the Incarnation. But they are very difficult subjects, and if any man has better ideas and can prove them from Holy Scriptures let his views be accepted rather than mine.'

There is one last aspect of Origen's teaching that we should consider: that is his view of the moral life of man. We have seen that he believed that human beings are put in this world to recover from the sin of which they have been guilty in an earlier spiritual existence. The aim set before them, according to Origen, is to recover their likeness to God. They have already been made in His image, an image that they have partly lost. It is their business to achieve a complete likeness to Him. In this effort they are absolutely free to choose for themselves. They will not be forced into the paths of goodness. They must exercise their own freedom of choice. But there is always the grace of God, given through Jesus, to help them. They have available all the power that they need to win success. This does not imply that all can expect to be perfect in this world. All indeed should use their capacities and abilities to the utmost, but Origen understands in a very realistic fashion the various capabilities of human beings. He divides sharply between the simple and the learned. The simple are the mere believers who cannot get beyond the limits of faith and who can never understand, for example, the allegorical explanation of the Scriptures. But the wise and learned are those who can get beyond the limits of mere belief to a state of scientific certainty and for whom the mystical explanation of Holy Scripture is easy and familiar territory.

This is a view to which we are not accustomed in these days; but there is one respect in which the circumstances of our own time have put us in much closer sympathy with Origen's thought. Our prosecution of what we conceive to be a just and righteous war, and the sufferings some of us may have had to undergo because of it, place us in circumstances very like those of the early Christians in time of persecution. Origen, so far from shrinking from such conditions, regards them as being almost ideal for the attainment of Christian virtue. One of his best known works is 'An Exhortation to Martyrdom.' In it he speaks in moving terms of the times when the normal instruction for baptism included a preparation for martyrdom; and that, he says, the candidates learnt to bear without being terrified or troubled at having to die for the living God. In those days, he continues, there was only a small number of believers, but they were truly faithful men and women who walked the straight and narrow way which leads to eternal life. Now that we have become more numerous, he adds, we must still try to imitate them. May we not believe that in this respect, too, Origen was a Pathfinder for us. It is in the sufferings of these present times that we shall learn to drink the Cup of which Jesus drank; and in so doing we shall learn the lessons for which this life was intended; and when we pass out of this school we shall enter upon our inheritance and reign with the King of kings.

3

ST. ATHANASIUS, DEFENDER OF
THE FAITH

THE name of Athanasius is perhaps as well known as that of any saint in the kalendar, because it is associated with the Athanasian Creed. As a matter of fact Athanasius had nothing to do with that so-called Creed. Nevertheless he was very largely responsible for another article of faith. That is the very important phrase 'of one substance with the Father,' which forms the central point of the formula we know as the Nicene Creed. Practically the whole of his life was taken up with the defence of that particular article of belief. So, in contrast with Origen, whom earlier we called a Pathfinder, I shall describe Athanasius as a Defender of the Faith.

He was born near the end of that third century which had witnessed the arduous academic labours of Origen, and he lived until nearly the last quarter of the fourth century, being about seventy-seven years old when he died. This longevity was extremely important, for it enabled him to see through from start to finish the tremendous controversy to which he dedicated his life and his powers.

His boyhood was passed at Alexandria. There is a picturesque story that he first attracted the attention of the Bishop of that place when, with some companions, he was playing on the sea shore. The bishop saw that they were playing ecclesiastical games, and Athanasius was pretending to preside as bishop over a baptism.

The prelate was so impressed by his gravity that he took him under his protection.

Whatever may be the truth of the story, it is certain that the Bishop did take the young Athanasius into his household. It was a wonderful opportunity for a bright lad. Alexandria was the second city and the greatest university of the contemporary world, and in the house of its Bishop (or Archbishop as he would be more properly called, for he was metropolitan with no fewer than a hundred bishops under him), the young boy would meet many of the most notable people of the day, including a number of heroic Christians who had suffered for their faith in the persecutions of the early part of the fourth century.

The boy must have used his opportunities to the utmost, because before he was twenty-one he had not only acquired a good education, but had himself published two small theological treatises, one of which, a book on the Incarnation, is still a standard work which has to be studied by the theological students in our Universities.

While still a young man Athanasius was ordained Deacon, and from being the secretary and companion of his Bishop very soon became Archdeacon, the most important ecclesiastical official in Alexandria next to the Bishop himself.

The appointment of this young defender of orthodox doctrine to such a position was especially interesting at that juncture, because there was even then arising a very great controversy on the subject of the Trinity. Arius, the priest in charge of Baucalis, one of the suburbs of Alexandria, had begun to teach that it was a mistake to speak of the Three Persons of the Blessed Trinity as equal to one another. He may have been trying to preserve the unity of God in order to win over some pagan philosophers, or perhaps as a protest against the surrounding polytheism, and he thought it would be much easier to insist upon that unity if you said that the Son and the Holy Spirit were really secondary deities and only God the Father was the one supreme Godhead.

You can imagine the amount of discussion that would be stirred up by such teaching. After there had been a great deal of quarrelling about it in Egypt the matter came to the ears of the Emperor Constantine. He had adopted Christianity and given it freedom from persecution because he hoped that it would bind all his vast dominions together. He could not afford in these circumstances to have quarrels among Christians themselves, and so he called a great Council at Nicea in 325, the first of what are known as the Oecumenical or General Councils, to settle the question.

The members of the Council were the Bishops from almost every part of the Christian world, but the protagonists on either side, who were allowed in the Council as assessors, were Arius and Athanasius. It would be difficult to imagine a greater contrast than that afforded by these two opponents. Arius was now an aged man, but a person of commanding presence, tall, grave, and with a great reputation for asceticism. Athanasius, on the other hand, was small and slight, but with beautiful features, and with the grace, if also the timidity and inexperience, of comparative youth.

It is impossible now, although it would be very interesting, to go through the details of the Council, but it must suffice to say that, under the advice of Athanasius, his Bishop and those who sympathized with him not only rejected the creed of Arius but also refused to accept any compromise that seemed to endanger the faith as they taught it. They felt that full belief in the divinity of

Christ could only be preserved by the acceptance of that phrase 'of one substance with the Father.' In the end their determination won the day, and by an overwhelming majority the vote of the Council went in their favour.

This success made Athanasius a marked man. Not long after the return to Alexandria, on the death of his patron, the Bishop, he was himself appointed to the vacant See. Thus, when he was not much over thirty, he became one of the most important ecclesiastical officers in the whole of the ancient world. He was to have a very troubled career and he was to go through many adventures and hair-breadth escapes, but for the first seven years he was left in comparative peace to carry on the work of his great province.

One of the most fruitful bits of work to which he set his hand during this period was the reorganization of the Church in Abyssinia. A certain Frumentius, who had been shipwrecked there, and had done considerable service before returning to Alexandria, pointed out the need for a Bishop and a more careful administration for those parts. Athanasius' reply was to ask who could better perform that task than Frumentius himself; and so he consecrated Frumentius as Bishop of Abyssinia and despatched him to carry on the work of organization.

After this period of peaceful work in Alexandria there was a fresh outbreak of the Arian heresy. The leaders of that school of thought were skilful politicians, and they were able to engineer a reaction against the uncompromising decision of the Council of Nicea. They could not at the moment attack the orthodox creed, but they could and did attack the most prominent of the Bishops who held it. One by one Athanasius saw his leading friends disappear, and then attention became centred upon himself. As the Arians dared not impugn his doctrine they tried to discredit him in the eyes of authority by bringing all sorts of charges against him.

One of the most interesting was that he had caused a certain presbyter, Arsenius, to be put to death in order that he might cut off his right hand and use it for magical purposes. The subsequent proceedings were as good as a detective story. When Athanasius was brought to trial a withered hand was certainly produced. But Athanasius turned to a shrouded figure that he had caused to be conducted into court. He lifted one corner of the cloak and exposed a right hand. Everybody became very interested. Is there any witness in court, he asked, who knew Arsenius? Yes, several replied, they knew him well. Athanasius drew the cloak from the figure. 'Is this your friend?' he asked. And they were obliged to admit that he was; alive and well, and with both hands intact. 'Who was it stole Arsenius' third hand?' asked Athanasius.

In spite of this momentary triumph other charges were brought against Athanasius, and finally the Emperor became frightened when it was alleged that the Bishop had used his position in Alexandria to delay the corn-ships carrying vitally necessary supplies to Rome. Then Athanasius was sent into exile—an experience that was to be repeated four times again before he came to the end of his life.

His second exile he spent in Rome, a matter of extreme importance for the Church, because he was able both to interest the Christians in Rome in his view of the orthodox faith and also to ensure that they understood and could describe in their Latin tongue the truths for which he was standing, and which in Greek had to be expressed in words that bore a superficially different meaning.

Also, he was able to introduce to the Latins a type of

Christian life that was new to them. Away in the Egyptian deserts a number of men, and even women, who desired to attain to a special state of holiness and live out the Christian life in what they believed to be its perfection, had isolated themselves in the desert. Athanasius was specially interested in this new lay movement, and he actually wrote a Life of the first great hermit, St. Anthony. Moreover, when he went to Rome he was accompanied by two men who had themselves practised this kind of asceticism. It was the first time that the inhabitants of Rome had met any one like them. They became keenly interested in this initial form of the monastic life; and that interest was the beginning from which the whole of Latin monasticism sprang.

In 346 Athanasius was allowed to return to his diocese, but he had not been there more than ten years before his enemies won the ear of the new Arian Emperor, and he was sent once more into exile. This time he spent six years in the desert, living with those hermits whom he had befriended and who now befriended him. He shared their life and their austerities. We have to picture this great administrator sitting like the poorest monk cross-legged upon the desert sand, with his writing materials on his knees and a heap of papyrus by his side, composing some of the books that were to establish his theological position and gain the adherence of the greater part of the Church.

But not always was he confined to the desert. Sometimes he would make an effort to get in touch with some part of his diocese or province that needed his personal superintendence. On one such occasion he shewed his presence of mind in a moment of danger. He was in a boat on the Nile when some friends overtook him and passed the word that a police boat was after him. Without a moment's hesitation he caused his own boat to be turned round to meet the police. When they came up to him they called out 'Have you seen anything of Athanasius?' 'Yes,' he replied, 'you are not far from him now,' and went on his way rejoicing, while the police dashed ahead to continue the fruitless search.

Athanasius was recalled to Alexandria at a time when a pagan Emperor was once again ruling over the Roman world. This was Julian the Apostate, who thought it would be a good way to discredit Christianity if he recalled all the exiled Bishops and set them to quarrel among themselves. Athanasius summoned a council of the Bishops in Alexandria. But instead of fulfilling the Emperor's expectations they were able to compose their differences and to consolidate the ranks of all who were sympathetic towards the Nicene faith. This did not suit Julian at all. Athanasius was once again banished, to return only on Julian's death.

When another persecuting Emperor succeeded, Athanasius was banished for the last time. He came back after the persecution was over, and then enjoyed seven peaceful years in great honour, watching over the gradual settlement of ecclesiastical differences and the growing unity of the Church, till at last he died in 373.

The character of Athanasius has been summed up by a modern theologian in these words:

Athanasius was not a great theologian nor was he a speculative thinker of high rank. But he had an unusually lucid and direct mind and he possessed the ability, by no means common among theologians, of distinguishing the essential from the unessential and going to the heart of the matter under discussion. Moreover, and this was the important thing, he had certain profound religious convictions that seemed to him threatened by Arius and his fellows, convictions that made up the very substance of Christianity as he understood it and distinguished it from all other religions the world had known.

His greatest service to Christianity was that he prevented speculation on the faith from deviating down a sidetrack which would have led ultimately to the complete ruin of specifically Christian belief. Christians must assert that there is only one God. They believe that the nature of this God is so rich that it can only be described under terms of multi-personality. There are three Persons in One God. That is the faith that Athanasius succeeded in impressing upon the Church for all time.

But Athanasius was interested not so much in strictly theological principles as in the actual salvation of human souls. That was his main interest from first to last. He would not tolerate any doctrine that would seem to jeopardize in the smallest degree our hold on the possibility of salvation. It was for this reason that he maintained that the Son of God who became man was fully and completely God and was no kind of intermediate being. The reason for this stand lay in the reason for the Incarnation itself. Why did the Son of God become Incarnate? asked Athanasius. And answered his own question with the striking affirmation, 'God became man in order that we might become God.' We 'become God' in so far as we are united with Christ. Through that unity with Him we are given power to become sons of God and are changed from glory to glory until we become like Him. Of course, the main point of the change from the angle of contemporary thought was that instead of being mortal we became immortal too like Christ. But the contention of Athanasius was that we could not be changed without union with Christ, and Christ could not effect that change unless he were so completely man as to be united with us in every part of our being, and so completely God as to change our mortal nature into that immortality which is characteristic of God.

I should like to conclude with one or two quotations from Athanasius' own writings, which will serve both to illustrate his style and to emphasize those elements of his teaching to which I have drawn attention.

The first is a delightful little analogy to point the moral that the likeness of God in man which has once been effaced can only be restored from the original.

When the likeness painted on a panel has been effaced by stains from without, he whose likeness it is must needs come once more to enable the portrait to be renewed on the same wood: for, for the sake of his picture, even the mere wood on which it is painted is not thrown away, but the outline is renewed upon it.

The second sums up the argument that no one but the divine and human Christ could suffice for the salvation of man.

It was in the power of none other to create anew the likeness of God's image for men, save the Image of the Father; and none other could render the mortal immortal, save our Lord Jesus Christ who is the very Life; and none other could teach men of the Father, and destroy the worship of idols, save the Word that orders all things and is alone the true only-begotten Son of the Father.

And the last illustrates the utter contempt of death manifested by those who had once grasped the reality of the Christian Faith.

But when they are gone over to Christ's faith and teaching, their contempt for death is so great that they even eagerly rush upon it, and become witnesses for the Resurrection the Saviour has accomplished against it. For while still tender in years they make haste to die, and not men only, but women also, exercise themselves by bodily discipline against it. So weak has Death become, that even women who were formerly deceived by him, now mock at him as dead and paralysed. For as when a tyrant has been defeated by a real king, and bound hand and foot, then all that pass by laugh him to scorn, buffeting and reviling him, no longer fearing his fury and barbarity, because of the king who has conquered him; so also, death having been conquered and exposed by the Saviour on the Cross, and bound hand and foot, all they who are in Christ, as they pass by, trample on him, and witnessing to Christ scoff at death, jesting at him, and saying what has been written against him of old: 'O death, where is thy victory? O grave, where is thy sting?'

That, then, is the story of Athanasius. I hope you will agree that I am right in calling him a Defender of the Faith. In defending the faith he shewed himself no finicky scholar making a lot of unnecessary to-do about mere words, but he preserved something that was of vital importance to you and me and to our hold upon Redemption.

4

ST. AMBROSE OF MILAN, THE STATESMAN

FOR the subject of my first talk I chose the first of the great Christian scholars. We found him in the East, that is, in the Greek-speaking half of the Christian world. Now we come to a very different kind of person, a man from the West, the Latin-speaking half of the Roman Empire.

It is true that, like Clement of Alexandria, Ambrose of Milan was reckoned a scholar. Indeed, together with Jerome, Augustine and Gregory, he is esteemed one of the four great Latin doctors of the Christian Church. He was also something of a poet and is accounted the father of Christian hymnody. However, it is not on these foundations that his greatest claim to fame rests, but rather on his ability as a statesman. With him we get the first of those great churchmen who were called upon to play a leading part not only in the sanctuary, but also in the arena of national affairs.

This arose quite naturally out of the circumstances of his birth and early training. He was born, as near as we can judge, in 340, a period when the great persecutions were over, and the Empire had made peace with the Church. His father was one of the most notable people in the Empire—the Governor of a vast district that covered the country which we now know as France, together with Britain and Spain. Ambrose was thus apprenticed to public service from his earliest days, and the fact that his parents were both Christians helped to make service the keynote of his character.

We have to picture to ourselves a very united family. There was a brother, Satyrus, to whom Ambrose was very devoted, and there was a sister, Marcellina, who later 'took the veil,' but as there was no convent for her to enter, she continued to live at home and bestowed the warmest care and affection upon her brothers. While Ambrose was still young his father died, but the boys received the best education the times could offer at Rome, and they then entered the profession of the Law, which was at that time, as now, the most frequented path to the high offices of State.

After he had qualified Ambrose practised in the court of the Praetorian Prefect of Italy, who was strongly attracted by the young man, and very soon gave him an important post as what I suppose we should call the 'Lieutenant Governor' of Liguria. It is said that when dismissing him to his new post, the Prefect became the author of an unconscious prophecy, for his last advice to him was, 'Go and conduct yourself not as a judge but like a Bishop.'

Milan was the headquarters of the area over which Ambrose presided. After a short time the Bishop of that place died. There was some controversy over the appointment of the successor, because at this time the Christian world was still split into two factions by the great heresy of Arianism, and both heretics and orthodox were anxious to get a nominee of their own into this very important See.

As the highest civil officer of the district, it was the duty of Ambrose to see that due order was kept. He went down to the church where the election was taking place to exhort the people to maintain a calm demeanour. The actual duty of the election fell to the local Bishops, but popular acclamation always carried great weight in the

D

proceedings. It so happened that soon after Ambrose entered the building a child's voice was heard to cry 'Ambrose for Bishop.' Instantly the whole congregation took up the cry, and the election of Ambrose was immediately decided upon.

This was by no means what Ambrose desired. It was a post from which he might well shrink, for he was not yet even baptized. That did not mean that he was not a serious and devoted Christian. It was often the custom at this period to receive children into the Church with a certain ceremony, but to postpone baptism until late in life. People had such a horror of sins committed after baptism that they were inclined to postpone the sacrament as long as possible. Ambrose was himself later to complain bitterly of this custom, but he had himself been a victim of it.

Also he might well have thought that the acceptance of such a post would mean the end of a most promising career, in which the very highest offices of State were open to him. Above all, there is no doubt that he felt himself on conscientious grounds unworthy of such an office.

He adopted some curious expedients to avoid consecration, not merely taking refuge in flight, but also acting in a very harsh and tyrannical manner when judging cases in the law courts in order to make people think that he was not at all the gentle sort of man they wanted. However, they were not to be put off, and he was first baptized and then consecrated.

For a man who had received only a civil training to have to occupy one of the most important sees in the West, at a time of great theological difficulty, might easily have turned out a tragedy. Ambrose says pathetically that he had to learn and teach at the same time. But he applied himself with such good effect to his studies that he was able to do very effective work for the Orthodox Faith.

This Faith, as we have seen, had been enunciated by Athanasius and accepted by the great Council of Nicea; but owing partly to the difficulty of understanding the terms employed, a Unitarian view was very widespread. Ambrose did good work in explaining the mind of the Eastern Church to the West, and so establishing a united front among the bulk of the Christians.

As Bishop he not only celebrated the Divine Mysteries every day, but preached at least every Sunday, and his sermons and lectures were written up in book form. The very fact that he came to theology as a lawyer and administrator perhaps gave him a manner of explaining Divine truth which was more useful for the times than the method of the highly cultured philosopher or metaphysician. Indeed, there is a strong opinion among certain sections of scholars to-day that he was actually responsible for the document which we now know as the Athanasian Creed. But there is considerable division upon this point, and the question remains open.

As soon as he became Bishop, Ambrose gave evidence of his sincerity by divesting himself of much of his very considerable personal property. A great part of it he gave to the Church or to the poor, and some he set aside to provide an income for his sister, Marcellina. The rest he put in charge of his brother Satyrus, so that he could give himself entirely to ecclesiastical affairs. Satyrus gave up an important post to come and live with Ambrose, the better to help him in the administration of his estate. But they were not destined to remain long together. In the pursuit of his business, Satyrus had to make a journey to North Africa, where he was wrecked in a storm, and endured such suffering that after his return he sank into a decline and died, a terrible blow both to Ambrose and his sister.

Ambrose added personal austerities to the sorrow inflicted upon him by the vicissitudes of life. It is recorded that he never ate any midday meal except on Saturdays and Sundays and other holy days. This frugality made it possible for him to engage more thoroughly in those works of charity which were not only dear to his heart but were abundantly necessary at that period.

The recent invasion by the Goths had resulted in the capture of many inhabitants of the Empire, who were then used as slaves. Ambrose set himself to purchase as many of these miserable wretches as possible and to restore them to their homes. To obtain funds for this work he did not refrain even from breaking up and selling the Sacramental vessels. 'If the Blood of Christ,' he said, 'redeems their souls, should not the vessels which hold that blood be used to redeem their bodies?' It will be seen that Ambrose was no haughty ecclesiastic, interested only in the aggrandizement of his own organization, but that he had a very real sympathy for his less fortunate fellow men.

We must remember that, when we think of his relations with the great rulers of his day. As Archbishop of this very important see he was brought into personal contact with successive Emperors. Although he never scrupled to oppose them when he felt that they were robbing the Church of its rights, he always endeavoured to serve their spiritual interests, and through them those of their people.

Perhaps the most difficult person with whom he had to deal was Justina, the mother of the young Emperor Valentinian II. As a sympathizer with the Arian heretics she desired to retain the use of one of the churches in

Milan for them. Ambrose felt that it would be a gross betrayal of his trust if he were to hand over a church for such a purpose. He filled the building with a vast congregation so that the soldiers could not take it by force. He then beguiled the tedium of the night watches by teaching them to sing antiphonally, that is, from side to side; a method which may have originated among the Jews and was certainly known in the East, but apparently had not been used in the Christian West until this time.

No less a person than Augustine, who had no love of florid music, described the great effect upon him of the chanting under Ambrose's leadership.

How I wept [he writes] at thy hymns and canticles, touched to the quick by the voices of thy melodious Church. The voices flowed into my ears, and the truth distilled into my heart, and thence there streamed forth a devout emotion, and my tears ran down, and I found relief therein.

The conversion of Augustine was the crowning glory of Ambrose's life. It happened in this way.

There had been a great controversy about the Altar of Victory in the Senate. The members had been accustomed to throw a few grains of incense on this altar as they took their places in the Senate House. But the Christians objected to the Altar as a pagan emblem and persuaded the Emperor to order its removal.

This led to one of the most famous debates in ancient history. Symmachus, the great pagan orator, defended the custom and Ambrose was the protagonist on the Christian side. In his defeat Symmachus looked round for some one who could rally the anti-Christian forces at Milan, and he sent to Africa for Augustine who was at that time a Manichee and the most famous of the rising orators of the day.

But on his arrival Augustine fell under the spell of

Ambrose. It is remarkable how often a man of first-rate ability can fall under the influence of a much less powerful intellect, when it is consecrated by a clear-sighted and single-hearted zeal. Augustine first began to admire the eloquence of Ambrose, and was then captivated by his teaching. After a very considerable mental struggle, which is beautifully described in the most famous passage of his Confessions, Augustine yielded to what he felt to be the call of God and became a Christian.

Perhaps the Emperor with whom the relations of Ambrose were most significant was Theodosius, who was much the ablest ruler of the period. On two occasions the Bishop felt himself obliged to resist this Emperor, and used his spiritual position to bring him to a better mind.

The first was when Theodosius had inflicted severe punishment upon a neighbouring Bishop, who in an excess of zeal had closed a Jewish synagogue. Ambrose, in the Emperor's presence, preached a sermon which was a thinly veiled exhortation to pardon those who had been caught in a manifest fault. As he came down from the pulpit Theodosius said to him, 'You have been preaching at me.' 'Only with a view to your advantage,' replied Ambrose. The Emperor said that he thought that the punishment had perhaps been too severe, but Ambrose, not satisfied, demanded a definite pardon, and it was only when he had got it in plain and unmistakable terms that he went on with the celebration of the Mysteries.

The second occasion was much more serious. The people of Thessalonica, in a fit of petulance, had murdered one of the Imperial officers. In retaliation the troops had beguiled the inhabitants into the Circus on the promise of some games, and there had put no fewer than seven thousand of them to death.

There was no doubt that Theodosius had consented to this appalling massacre, if, indeed, he had not instigated it. Ambrose wrote to him, moving him to repentance, and pointing out that without such repentance it would be impossible to consecrate the Eucharist in the Emperor's presence. In the end Theodosius not only professed his penitence, but did public penance and was restored to the fellowship of the Church.

Those then are the chief events in the life of St. Ambrose. What may we say was his great achievement? Surely this, that under the providence of God he was one of the instruments by which was made possible the transition from the old Pagan world to the Christian civilization of the Middle Ages. By his conversion of Augustine, and his gallant stand against the wilfulness of the half-tamed Emperors, he helped to introduce a new order of Christian peace and service. But this would not have been possible if he had not been himself a wholly devoted servant of Christ. This is what gives him his title to be accounted a saint. Of the intensity of his religious life we have abundant evidence in his hymns, and of that we have no better expression than in his beautiful ode to the Creator, with a quotation from which I will conclude:

> O Strength and Stay upholding all creation,
>   Who ever dost Thyself unmoved abide,
> Yet day by day the light in due gradation
>   From hour to hour through all its changes guide;
>
> Grant to life's day a calm unclouded ending,
>   An eve untouched by shadows of decay,
> The brightness of a holy death-bed blending
>   With dawning glories of the eternal day.

5

ST. GREGORY, THE GREAT PRELATE

IN discussing the lives of certain saints and leaders of the Christian Church we have seen how varied is the character of sainthood. I want now to consider another example—that of the statesman and administrator, Gregory the Great.

There are, of course, many Gregorys who have won renown in Christian history, but this is the Gregory whom we all remember by the story of the fair-haired English slave-boys in the market-place at Rome, whom he described as not Angles but Angels. The story reveals the kindly and witty ecclesiastic; but it is also typical of one who was 'perhaps the ablest Prelate and probably the best man who ever sat on the Chair of Peter.'

Of his virtue and ability we shall see many instances, but of his quiet wit I may record straightaway two other instances. One, where he is describing the way in which he wrote the greatest of his books. He speaks of the words of advice given him by his own monks, 'words of advice,' he adds in parenthesis, 'which were sufficiently numerous.' The other in a passage where he is consoling a brother bishop who had tried in vain to convert a certain pagan. 'Never mind,' he said, 'you will get your reward. The negro comes out of the baths as black as he went in, yet the bath attendant gets his pay.'

This mild and pleasant quality will give us a special interest from the outset in one to whom we English-speaking Christians owe a very great deal.

Gregory was born in the middle of the sixth century of an aristocratic Christian family. He was educated for the Civil Service, and by the time he was thirty-three he had already attained to the topmost rung of the department within the city of Rome, and had become Prefect, that is the chief officer, of the city. It was a period of great anxiety in the history of the Empire, reminding us of the condition of much of Europe to-day. Rome had been several times overrun by the Barbarians, and although it could never be so completely destroyed as a modern city can be by bombing from the air, yet many of its buildings were lying in ruins.

We have reason to believe that Gregory fulfilled his duties with conspicuous ability, or he could never have gained the confidence and popularity that were so conspicuously his. But his post never held the foremost place in his mind. He had long desired to give himself up completely to the service of God, and for Gregory that meant nothing less than life in a monastery. Already two of his aunts had become nuns, and when his father died his widowed mother followed their example.

Gregory felt the time had now come when he could change his own manner of life. He had inherited considerable wealth from his father, but he used it all in the building of six monasteries in the country and a seventh in Rome. The latter was the Monastery of St. Andrew, of which he himself became a member. The citizens of Rome were profoundly moved at the sight of one who had formerly appeared in the city in the silken robes and jewels of a Prefect now clothed in the coarse beggar's garb of a monk.

For a few years Gregory lived a life of the greatest austerity, carrying his asceticism so far as permanently to ruin his health. But a man of his attainments and experience was too useful to the administrative life of the Church to be allowed to bury himself in obscurity, and presently the Pope of the day ordained him deacon and made him one of the seven Archdeacons who were the principal ecclesiastical officers in the city.

The following year the Pope sent him to Constantinople as a kind of ambassador. This was an extremely important post, because Constantinople was at this time the seat of the Empire, the place where the Roman Emperor lived and had his Court. Once again Gregory proved himself a most efficient officer, but he lamented the loss of the contemplative life. The only thing that made the change at all palatable for him was that some of his monks had followed him and lived with him in the palace allotted for his use. There they reproduced their monastic life as closely as possible, and Gregory spent many happy hours lecturing to them.

These lectures have come down to us in his greatest book, the *Magna Moralia*, or Book of Morals, developed in the form of a commentary on the Book of Job. In the introduction there is a pathetic reference to Gregory's own ill-health. He says that he is never free from pain, and he points out how difficult that makes the task of writing a book. The body is the instrument of the mind and if the body is not in good shape the mind can no more use it effectively than a musician can produce sound melody from a broken instrument. But after all, he says, that may give him a special sympathy with the subject of his lectures.

Perchance it was this that Divine Providence designed, that I, a stricken one, should set forth Job stricken, and that by these scourges I should more perfectly enter into the feelings of one that was scourged.

Incidentally, those of us who are not good at languages

may derive some comfort from the fact that in spite of his residence at the Greek capital Gregory was never able to master the Greek tongue. St. Augustine had had the same difficulty before him, and it is a curious fact that ability to master foreign tongues seems to have no relation whatever to ability in other directions, whether of an academic or practical kind.

After seven years of this life Gregory returned to Rome to become Abbot of his own monastery of St. Andrew. It was then that he had his adventure with the slave boys, and made up his mind that the English people must be converted to Christianity. He desired to undertake this task himself, and had actually started on his way, when the plan was discovered by the Roman populace and their outcry induced the Pope to recall him.

After three years as Abbot of St. Andrew's, during which time he became recognized as the leading ecclesiastic in Rome, Gregory was brought into special prominence through an outbreak of bubonic plague. The Pope himself was carried off by that visitation. Gregory was elected into his place, but while they were still awaiting confirmation of the election from Constantinople the plague became so bad that Gregory organized a tremendous series of processions to sing Litanies as a special act of intercession for relief from the plague. It is said that as the procession reached the mausoleum of Hadrian Gregory saw a vision of the angel of the plague sheathing his sword as a sign that the pestilence was to cease. It was from that incident that the building got the name by which it has ever since been known, the Castle of St. Angelo.

The procession in itself is of great historic interest because it reveals to us something of the contemporary condition of the Church in Rome. Each of the seven

Archdeaconries provided its own contingent—the first the Abbesses and Nuns, the second the children, the third the married women, the fourth the Abbots and Monks, the fifth the widows, the sixth the clergy, and the seventh the laymen. Each party started from a separate church, and met together at the Basilica of St. Mary, where the final service was held. It can be imagined what an impression this imposing ceremonial must have made upon the Barbarians and other visitors to the city. It was by such means that ecclesiastical Rome took the place of the old pagan centre of the civilized world.

Gregory became Pope in 590, and as the Emperor was at Constantinople at the other end of the Mediterranean and the civil government was very inefficient, it was left to Gregory to act not only as the ecclesiastical but also as the secular head of the people of Rome. It fell to him to negotiate peace with the Lombards, who were still pressing upon the city. The civil authorities might complain of the Pope's interference, but they were compelled to honour his peace, and every one knew that but for him the condition of the city would have been deplorable indeed.

Not only did he negotiate peace with the Barbarians, but he also managed with supreme ability the Papal estates. The Church was at this time the greatest landowner in Italy, and the greatest taxpayer. It was therefore of the utmost importance that its estates should be well managed, and during Gregory's time they were a model to every landowner in the country.

Gregory's interest stretched out beyond the Eternal City and its immediate environment. He was in touch with the Church in all parts of the civilized world, and humility and dignity were nicely blended in his relations with the more important of his colleagues overseas. When the Patriarch of Alexandria called Gregory his superior and wrote of his 'commands' Gregory replied that they were both on an equal footing, and that he was not giving commands but only advice. On the other hand when John the Faster, Patriarch of Constantinople, assumed the title of Oecumenical, or Universal Bishop, Gregory was very shocked and said that no Bishop ought to assume such a title. For his own part Gregory was satisfied with the title which he made peculiarly his own, 'Servus Servorum Dei,' 'the Servant of the Servants of God.'

One country Gregory never forgot in the midst of his care for all the Churches, and that was England. On the failure of his early scheme he had decided to buy a number of English slaves and train them to go back as missionaries to their own people. But now that he was Pope it was possible for him to do something better. He commissioned the Prior of his own monastery of St. Andrew's, Augustine, to set out with a number of monks to convert the country. He chose a time when he was on particularly good terms with the Franks, and when Ethelbert the King of Kent had married a Frankish Christian Princess. Augustine, with his monks, duly set out; but after a few days they were so perturbed by stories of what the Saxons would do with them when they arrived in England that they sent him back to Gregory asking for the abandonment of the mission. But Gregory fortified him with fresh letters of commendation to the various princes, gave him a little more authority, and bade him continue the expedition. That is how Augustine and his band of monks landed in Kent in 597, and the conversion of Southern England was begun.

This was perhaps the brightest jewel in Gregory's crown. But what he did for England he did in a certain measure for other countries too. He assisted the whole of

Europe to pass out of the old era, whether of barbarism or of classical culture, into the new era of the Middle Ages, and he did it mostly through Christianizing the means of administration. Just as Augustine of Hippo handed on the old classical literary culture impregnated with Christianity, so Gregory took the old Roman genius for government and infused it into the ecclesiastical organization. Since the Church was the teacher of the Barbarians it was thus Gregory who became largely responsible for that European Christian civilization of which we are the heirs to-day, and which is now seriously threatened for the first time in fifteen hundred years.

But it is not for his tremendous administrative ability that Gregory has been most honoured by the Church. More attention has been paid to his prominence as a teacher, and he has been reckoned the last of the four great Latin 'doctors' of the Church. Yet he was not really a scholar. He had no interest in learning or philosophical study for themselves. His sole interest was in edification, in building up the spiritual and moral life of God's people. For this very reason he occupies a unique position in the history of Christian thought. While he contributed nothing new out of his own native genius to the sum total of Christian doctrine, what he did was to gather up the popular religion of his day and lend to it an authority which made it the received religion for many centuries afterwards. It was there that his special contribution lay. English critics used to say that Mr. Asquith was a peculiarly useful speaker, because he was always able to point out to people clearly what was latent in their own minds. In much the same way Gregory made the Christian world of his day consciously aware of its own method of presenting the Christian religion to itself.

We cannot look in his case for the boldly speculative theology of an Origen, nor even for a clear recognition of what is essential in the Faith such as was characteristic of Athanasius. Gregory's horizon was far more limited than theirs. He had not their interest in the great thinkers of the past. The whole of the classical pagan literature, whether Greek or Latin, he entirely eschewed. It was sufficient to him to read the Bible and the Fathers of the Christian Church. Anything else seemed unworthy of a follower of Christ.

He was thus without any saving pinch of the salt of cynicism. He began a period of extraordinary credulity in the Christian Church. He wrote one book, *The Dialogues*, which consists almost entirely of stories of miracles connected with the raptures of the Saints and the curious devices of demons. He developed the theory that the Son of God had assumed human flesh in order that He might trick the Devil into thinking that He was a mere man and so deal with Him as justice only allowed him to do with a sinful human being. Thus the Devil, having transgressed his own limits, could be honourably destroyed. In Gregory too we get the careful charting out of the region beyond death, with precise details as to residence in purgatory and so on.

In many respects Gregory's religion was the kind of religion that people of my own generation remember being taught when they were tiny children. To whatever ecclesiastical colour they belonged, whether catholic or evangelical, the substratum of thought was the same, and to us nowadays it seems almost sub-Christian. It is curious how the modern mind has gone back beyond Gregory, and even beyond Augustine, until it finds thinkers like Origen and Clement more to its liking.

In one respect Gregory had learnt from Origen. He

read the Bible in much the same way, finding in it not only an historical sense, but also an allegorical and a moral interpretation. You can see this at once when you read his great commentary on Job.

He begins with the first verse. 'There was a man in the land of Uz whose name was Job.' Why, he asks, are we told that Job lived in the land of Uz? Because that was the land of the Gentiles, and we are told what was Job's environment in order that we may understand him better. His virtue stands out all the brighter for being shewn against the black background of paganism. That is an acute piece of criticism, and Gregory goes on like that for the first five verses shewing the historical meaning of the words.

Then he starts all over again to find the allegorical meaning. 'There was a man in the land of Uz whose name was Job.' What is the allegorical meaning of this? Surely it is to be found in the fact that the name 'Job' means 'a mourner,' one who grieves. And does not that remind us at once of the passage in Isaiah—'Surely he hath borne our griefs and carried our sorrows'? Obviously therefore Job is but a type of the Messiah, the suffering Christ who was to come. So again we go through the five verses, finding an allegorical meaning in every phrase.

And then we start once again to get, this time, the moral meaning. 'There was a man in the land of Uz whose name was Job.' What is the moral lesson we may draw from this? Surely if the name Job signifies grieving, it is a lesson to us that we must grieve for the sinfulness and transitoriness of this life as we make our way towards eternity. It is only as we are dissatisfied with the present that we shall really long for something better and higher in the future. That is an example of the way in which the

Bible was interpreted by the leading exponent of the day.

Gregory was interested not only in Biblical exegesis but also in many practical questions. He wrote a book on Pastoral Care, which like the other book I have mentioned, and the third called *The Dialogues*, was widely read throughout the Middle Ages, and probably did far more than the great philosophical works of Thomas Aquinas to frame the thoughts and religion of everyday people.

That he was interested in Church music we know from the fact that his name has been given to a particular type of chanting, though actually how much he had to do with it is doubtful. That he was interested in the actual conduct of services we know from the fact that a famous prayer book, *The Gregorian Sacramentary*, is also known by his name. Again we are not certain how much in it is actually due to his own personal impress, but we can be satisfied that like most of the Bishops of his day he did strive to set a standard in liturgical matters by instructing not only the lay people but also the young clergy and students for the ministry with whom he came in contact. We have seen how even in Constantinople he lectured to his monks, and there can be no doubt that he strove to set the highest standard of clerical life and practice before all those who were initiated by him into the clerical office.

It was here that his great administrative ability and his qualities as a teacher would join together to spread his influence throughout the whole of Latin Christendom.

But for you and me, English-speaking Christians, Gregory will be remembered not merely as a great ecclesiastical administrator, nor as the last of the Latin teachers, but as the Bishop who sent his friend to bring the Gospel to our home land. Gregory is for us above all what the old English writers loved to call him, 'Our Father who gave us baptism.'

E

6

ST. BERNARD OF CLAIRVAUX, MONASTIC
LEADER

I AM going to ask you to skip four centuries, and think with me about St. Bernard. There are, of course, several Saints of this name, and you must not think that the Bernard about whom I am going to speak has anything to do with St. Bernard dogs. You will get him clear if you attach to him the name of the monastery, Clairvaux, where he spent nearly the whole of his life.

There are two respects in which Bernard of Clairvaux resembles one of our earlier heroes, Ambrose of Milan. He was a very great figure in national, and indeed in international affairs, and he was also something of a hymn writer. But these two similarities apart, the two men afford a great contrast. Ambrose was primarily a man of affairs. Bernard was first and foremost a monk. That is how he wished to be known, and that gives the keynote to his life and character. He never seems to have had any other ambition.

He was born in 1091. Both his father and mother belonged to knightly families, and both were renowned for the depth and sincerity of their religion. There were seven children—six boys and one girl. Bernard was the third son. His elder brothers followed the usual knightly career and they were generally at war when they were not hunting. Their life made no appeal to Bernard. But he, no less than they, was a true child of his age, a definitely medieval figure. He realized the tremendous contrast between the coarseness and violence of life in the world and the peace and sublimity of life in the cloister.

It was the great age of Monasticism, when the successive reforms of the Cluniacs and the Cistercians had impressed upon the minds of men the splendour of the ascetic ideal. Indeed, the monastic life had come to be looked upon as the essential Christianity. Conversion, a word which is now often on our lips, meant then nothing but the turning from the world to enter a monastery. It was within the walls of the convent that salvation was most secure, and to ensure their salvation men would take monastic vows even on their death-bed.

There is small wonder then that Bernard, revolted by the thought of continual fighting, turned to the monastic life as the only alternative. It was indeed the only alternative for so ardent a mind as his. It is significant that his conversion took place when he was on a visit to his father and brothers, who were characteristically at that time laying siege to a neighbouring castle. It was also typical that he should decide to enter the severest monastery of the period, the Abbey of Citeaux, which had pitched the standard of austerity so high that after its first initial success it was beginning to fail for lack of recruits.

It was further typical of his ardour that when he went he did not go alone. He persuaded his brothers (those of them who were old enough) and even his father to join him and they gathered with them such a number of friends that it was a band of thirty that finally offered itself to the amazed and overjoyed Abbot of Citeaux.

There Bernard rapidly distinguished himself by his zeal and by his obvious power of influencing others. He had not been there very long before the membership had grown to such an extent that it became possible, and indeed

necessary, to found daughter houses. It was determined to
set up one such house in a certain valley, which had been a
noted resort of robbers and had borne the ominous name
of The Valley of Wormwood, but later became known as
The Beautiful Valley, or Clairvaux.

When a little band of monks was sent out to found this
new home, Bernard, although he was the youngest, was
placed in charge. The brethren had first to build a
shelter for themselves, and then to provide for their own
sustenance. It can easily be imagined how hard their
lot must have been. Frequently they were near to starva-
tion, and there were some who wished to give up the
attempt and return to the Mother House. But Bernard,
with his great religious enthusiasm, rallied the waverers
and shamed them by his own endurance. The Abbey of
Clairvaux gradually established itself and grew in numbers
until it became one of the most famous of the French
monasteries. Indeed, during his own lifetime, Bernard
saw the establishment of no fewer than sixty-eight
daughter Houses in eleven different countries.

In all our consideration of his other activities, we must
remember that the strain of management and direction
of the affairs of his monastery remained constant throughout Bernard's life. That meant not only the supervision
of a vast business organization, but also the intimate care
of individuals. Clairvaux became the training centre
for many of the rising young men of the day, and Bernard
was never happier than when he was dealing personally
with his Novices. During his own lifetime he saw one
Pope, six Cardinals, and thirty Bishops appointed from
among the men trained in his own monastery.

Over and above the influence he thus exerted, he was
a very important figure in the Church as a whole. He
soon became renowned as a writer, an orator, and a saint,

as well as a wise counsellor in all practical affairs. There was no Pope of the day who exercised anything like so powerful an influence as did Bernard.

Certainly that influence was badly needed, for Christendom was torn asunder by a schism in the Papacy. There were two rival claimants to the Papal dignity, and the history books are very largely taken up with the story of the quarrels that ensued. All we need do is to remember that Bernard espoused the cause of Innocent II, and after long years of strife and argument, involving many journeys through nearly the whole of Western Europe, succeeded in getting his candidate universally accepted.

Naturally the influence gained in this campaign made the name of Bernard respected far and wide. Kings and nobles found it wise to listen to his advice, and men of lesser degree followed him because he was a devout and humble saint. We are told that on a journey to Milan crowds of every class and station came to see him.

Nobles and lowly born, knights and foot-men, burghers and poor, streamed from their homes in separate companies to greet the man of God. All alike were delighted to gaze upon him; they who could hear his voice accounted themselves most fortunate. Multitudes kissed his feet; and although it pleased him ill, yet did he not reason with or forbid men prostrate in devotion to his person. When they could, they even plucked threads and tore strips from his garments as remedies for the sick, judging that whatever he had touched or used was thereby sanctified.

There is indeed no doubt about the many cures performed by the Saint. We may nowadays explain his extraordinary gift of healing on psychological grounds. He himself believed that he had the power of working miracles, and in more than one critical situation he staked his whole cause on his success in some such act. But what

I have already said about his curious influence over his brothers and the others who followed him to Citeaux will make it perhaps easier to understand how such a reputation could be quite genuinely gained.

His influence was seen again when the Pope determined on the second Crusade. Bernard was the person who was sent all over the country to preach that Crusade, and his was the eloquence which stirred many thousands to take the Cross and launch themselves into a campaign that was to cost a large percentage of them their lives.

The second Crusade was a miserable failure; but that was no fault of Bernard's. It was a bitter blow to him; but he had no hesitation in ascribing it to the sin of the participants. The candid reader of history will probably agree that Bernard's judgement was correct. There was much sheer nobility and religious devotion among the Crusaders, but there was far more jealousy, rivalry and utter ineptitude mingled with downright wickedness.

Bernard realized that in this kind of warfare holiness was as necessary as bravery. He sought to combine the two virtues in a new foundation, that of the Knights Templars—'The Poor Fellow-soldiers of Christ and of the Temple of Solomon' as they called themselves.

The formation of this Order was a matter of great importance for the whole history of Europe. It involved the establishment of a regular armed force, not mercenary, yet independent of external control. Such an institution cut right across the structure of medieval feudalism and was fraught with great possibilities for good and evil alike. Whether or not the actual Rule of the Knights Templars was drawn up by Bernard, it is certain that he was largely responsible for the spirit by which the Order was animated.

Not only was Bernard concerned with these elements

of what one might call external history, but he was also vastly interested in contemporary thought. One of the best known controversies in medieval times arouse out of his clash with Abelard. This is the teacher whose name is so well known at the present time, not so much for his philosophical ability as for his romantic association with Heloise. The two men represent opposite poles in spiritual life, both of which are necessary, but each of which is often thought to be incompatible with the other. Bernard was all fire and glow and warmth. For him the old traditional statements were enough. To begin to worry one's head by looking into the foundations of things might only produce doubts for oneself and distress for the Church at large. Abelard, on the other hand, possessed a cold, clear, critical intellect. He was never satisfied to accept anything at its face value, but was always anxious to examine the cause of things, and to follow the argument wherever it might lead. His ambition was to understand in order that he might believe.

The passion of the one man was love; the passion of the other was truth. When it came to a public disputation, Abelard, apparently thinking that the meeting had been, as we should say, 'framed,' made no reply, but appealed to Rome. Although he suffered a technical defeat, his influence lasted long in the medieval church, and indeed it may be said that even the great system of Thomas Aquinas could never have been built up if it had not been for the preliminary work of Abelard.

Happily the influence of Bernard lived on side by side with that of his opponent. It is with us to-day in some of the hymns that are ascribed to him. It is doubtful whether they actually proceeded from his pen, but there can be no doubt that the spirit they breath is that of

Bernard. Two of them are very well known to us and they glow with a warmth of heart-felt piety which reveals what consolation Bernard drew from his religion. One is the beautiful Passiontide hymn:

> O Sacred Head, sore wounded,
>> Defiled and put to scorn;
> O Kingly Head surrounded
>> With mocking crown of thorn.

The other is frequently sung at all seasons of the Christian year:

> Jesu, the very thought of Thee
>> With sweetness fills the breast;
> But sweeter far Thy face to see,
>> And in Thy presence rest.

One wonders how often Bernard whispered these words with a sigh while he was busy about the affairs of his far-flung monastic organization, or was trying to appease a divided Europe, or battling with what he believed to be heresy, or rousing troops of Crusaders to fight against the Saracen. But we may be sure that his only desire in all those duties was to serve his Master, and it is certain that in God's will he found his peace.

7

ST. FRANCIS, LOVER OF ANIMALS

THE reason for St. Francis' popularity is not far to seek. He is often described as the most Christ-like figure that the Church has ever possessed. The ages immediately succeeding to his own perceived this similarity just as clearly as we do to-day. They expressed it in their own characteristic fashion by building up legends about his early years, which made his life appear a replica of that of Jesus of Nazareth. So he was said to have been born in a stable and to have undergone many experiences which were in reality those of Christ.

Another reason for his popularity is that there is also, paradoxical as it may seem, a striking note of modernity in the life and teaching of St. Francis. Chesterton points out that 'he anticipated all that is most liberal and sympathetic in the modern mood; the love of nature; the love of animals; the sense of social compassion; the sense of the spiritual dangers of prosperity and even of property.'

It may be said of him that we love him as we do our Lord Himself, because while his life would be impossible to reproduce in detail under modern conditions, yet his character and ideals represent the inmost longing of all our hearts.

He was born in the little Italian town of Assisi in 1182, the son of a well-to-do cloth merchant. Francis was his nickname, meaning 'Frenchie.' Little Frenchie was so called because his father had visited France and had his son taught the language of that country, no doubt thinking that it might be of advantage for trade. But what St. Francis himself seems to have got out of it was a knowledge of the French troubadours and their songs, and not least of their spirit, which to a large extent informed his own and which he later translated into a joyous religious devotion.

He spent a gay and somewhat reckless youth. He saw service in the army and for a year was a prisoner of war. He seems, however, to have had spasmodic longings for a fuller satisfaction than material ambitions could bring, and there was a period of doubt and hesitation such as most geniuses experience before they discover their life's work. Several stories illustrate his search for higher things.

Meeting a professional soldier, worn and weary and very down-at-heel, he tore off his own resplendent uniform, handed it to the officer, and so preserved the dignity of knightly chivalry. Again, one evening he was revelling with his companions. When supper was over, the merry party dashed out of the hot, lighted room into the open air. The dark indigo-blue vault of heaven was overhead, besprent with myriads of stars, the air was soft and balmy, and all was hushed. Francis stood still, his sensitive, poetic nature touched by the contrast. 'What ails you, Francis?' asked one of the revellers. 'He is star-gazing for a wife,' joked another. 'Ah!' said Francis solemnly, 'for a wife past all that your imaginations can conceive!' His soul, filled by the music of the troubadours, with inarticulate cravings, strained for some great love to fill it and satisfy it, but what that love was he did not yet know.

The crisis was reached when he believed himself to have received a Divine command to rebuild the ruined chapel of San Damiano. To get sufficient money he not

only sold his own horse, but a number of bales of his
father's cloth. For this the irate father brought him
before the Bishop's court. There the young man realized
with a sudden clarity that if he was to pursue his ideals
he must leave his father and all that he had. With his
usual impetuous literalness he made his intention clear
by stripping off the very clothes that he wore, placing
the money he had received for the cloth on the top of
the pile, and so returning everything that he owed to his
father before leaving him for ever.

In his half-naked condition outside the court he accepted
a rough peasant's smock, and so almost by accident
established the Habit of the Order he was to found.
Having no visible means of subsistence he had to live
by begging, while he continued the work of rebuilding
the church with his own hands.

Then in 1208 this critical period of his life was brought
to an end when he was struck by the words of the Gospel
read during service in Chapel, 'Provide neither gold, nor
silver, nor brass in your purses, nor scrip for your journey,
neither two coats, neither shoes, nor yet staves; and as ye
go, preach, saying, the kingdom of heaven is at hand.'

'Here is what I wanted,' said Francis, and leaving the
church, in his impulsive and symbolic way he threw off
his shoes, cast away his staff, and replaced his leathern
girdle by a piece of cord. Thus, again by accident, he
completed the uniform of his Order.

His first two disciples were from most unlikely classes—
a wealthly merchant and a cathedral dignitary. The
numbers began to increase, and he sought the permission
first of his Bishop, and then of the Pope, to organize them
into a solid body.

It was a difficult proposal and probably no one realized
its great consequences for the future of the Church, and

indeed of the world. Monasticism, as hitherto known in the Western world, had been an eminently respectable, not to say aristocratic movement. Here was a man who wanted to preserve the same vows of chastity, obedience and poverty as the monks, but wished to make poverty a sterner reality than others had yet done. His followers were to 'live to preach, and beg to live.' They were to be not only the friends of the outcast and poor, but actually to live like them. Their poverty would be even greater than that of their hearers. They were mostly laymen and not clergy. Francis himself never went beyond Deacon's Orders. And they looked the veriest scarecrows. Pope Innocent III was hardly willing to entertain this strange offer of help, but in the end he gave his bare permission and with this sanction the work went forward.

The Little Brothers, as they called themselves, set to work to restore another church in Assisi, the Church of the Portiuncula, which soon became famous as the home of the Order; while the already restored St. Damian's became the home of a body of women following the same ideals under the guidance of St. Clare.

The brothers' life was of the simplest, and Francis would not even allow them to own a Prayer Book. They were for the most part untrained laity, unaccustomed to the long canonical Hours of the Clergy, but they were expected when they came in sight of any church the say the Lord's Prayer together with the prayer St. Francis taught them: 'We adore Thee, O Christ, in all Thy churches which are in all the world, and we bless Thee because Thou hast by Thy holy cross redeemed the world.' These two prayers formed the only special Office they had.

In 1215 there was held the famous Council of the Lateran which was attended by St. Francis, and where he not only received official recognition but also met St. Dominic, the founder of the other great Order of Friars.

Now occurs the happiest period of St. Francis' life. He had launched his great work. It was developing daily and was not yet disturbed by faction. It is to this period that belong many of the instances of St. Francis' curious sympathy for and intimacy with animals. Evelyn Underhill says of him: 'The whole life of St. Francis of Assisi, that spirit transfigured in God, who loved above all other birds a certain little bird which is called the lark, was one long march to music through the world. Every one knows how he preached to his little sisters, the birds. He availed himself of the kindly offices of the falcon, enjoyed the friendship of the pheasant, soothed the captured turtle doves, his simple-minded sisters, innocent and chaste.'

It is related that 'the blessed Francis, returning from beyond the sea, was travelling through the Marches of Venice, and heard a vast multitude of birds singing among the bushes. And when he saw them he said to his companions, "Our sisters, the birds, are praising their Maker. Let us then go into their midst and sing to the Lord the Canonical Hours." And when they had gone into their midst, the birds moved not from the place; but as, on account of their chirping and twittering, the brethren were not able to hear each other, the holy men turned to the birds and said, "Sisters, cease your song until we have rendered our bounden praise to God." And they at once were silent, and when the praises were finished resumed their song.'

Francis seems to have been a true 'animal man,' in the sense that all wild creatures felt at ease in his presence. It is told how at different times a leveret and a wild rabbit took refuge from their pursuers in his clothing.

Always he felt some revelation of God to be conveyed through both the flora and fauna of the created world, and sometimes he was able to make the lesson explicit in the most child-like way. Thus the story is told how he found a motherless lamb and led it through the villages, and even the cities along his route, using it as an object lesson of the white purity of the Lamb of God. It was in a similar spirit that he devised the Christmas Crib with its attendant ox and ass and obtained permission for it to be set up in churches.

But we should make a mistake if we idealized the life of St. Francis to such an extent that we thought of him as if he were always at peace among his flowers and his birds. On the contrary his life was beset not only with hardship, but what is much more difficult to bear, disagreement with his own followers. But through it all he pursued his revolutionary ideals.

He was perhaps the only person of his time to understand the true Christian attitude towards the unbeliever. It was the period of the Crusades, when the only instrument used by Christians to convert the infidel was the sword. Francis, on the other hand, made several unavailing attempts to proclaim the Gospel in peaceful fashion. On one occasion he left the Crusading army to penetrate alone and unarmed into the camp of the Sultan. The Sultan recognized his genuine piety and gentleness, and although he did not yield to his persuasions he returned him unharmed to his friends.

It was on his return from this expedition that Francis received his first great shock with regard to the course pursued by members of his own Order. When he went to visit his friend Cardinal Ugolino, he found his friars living in a splendid house which had been furnished for them by a wealthy person of the neighbourhood. He ordered them all out, the sick as well as the whole, and it was only under the persuasions of the Cardinal that he allowed even the sick to be returned to their beds. His followers claimed that they had not departed from the rule of poverty, because they did not own the building but only had the use of it. The division of opinion remained until his death and for many long years afterwards, some desiring to accommodate their methods to the normal world, while others desired to remain literally in the extremity of poverty.

The latter fell ultimately into heresy, because, as Chesterton says, they set the mood against the mind. That is to say, they took the ideal of St. Francis, and, identifying it with the actual details by which it was expressed, tried to mould not only their own private lives but the organization of their vast society in strict accordance with the same details.

It is, of course, an age-long difficulty, experienced by all the followers of Christ, and will endure so long as we are compelled to live in the world. There can be no doubt that there are individuals who are called upon to surrender all possessions for the sake of their religion; but a great organization cannot do that because if it did it would have no more means of carrying out its work than the artisan who has thrown his tools into the river. Every organization must have its plant and machinery and that involves the ownership of property by some one. So even the professed disciples of St. Francis found that the right way of following him was to cultivate his inner spirit of renunciation; to imitate his love for his fellow men, for animals and for all created things; and to acquire that troubadour's light and cheerful gaiety which made of even the hardest religious activities a joy and a delight.

8

SAVONAROLA, THE PREACHER OF RIGHTEOUSNESS

IT is a Sunday morning towards the end of the fifteenth century, and the scene is laid in the great duomo, or Cathedral, of Florence. The nave is filled with a surging mass of humanity and in the pulpit a friar in the Dominican habit is preaching. He has a hooked nose, full lips, and thin cheeks. His rather staring eyes flash with fire, and his impassioned utterance whips up the growing excitement of the crowd. It is Girolama Savonarola, preaching the last of his Advent sermons for the year.

He is denouncing the iniquity of Florence and proclaiming God's punishment for its sins. He has seen a vision—a hand bearing a sword, descending out of heaven and holding the point over the city. Upon it are engraved the words, 'The sword of the Lord will come soon and quickly upon the earth.' His hearers are so moved by this and his other utterances that they determine to clean up their city. A medal is struck showing the vision on the one side and the head of the friar on the other, and a new reformed life henceforth characterizes the citizens of Florence.

This prophetic preacher of righteousness had come into the world at a critical period. Only a year after his birth the Turks had captured Constantinople and threatened the overthrow of Christian civilization. From within also the civilization was threatened. The culture of Europe was beginning to suffer an upheaval owing to the birth of a new learning. The old Christian standards which for 1,000 years or more had seemed so certain were being questioned, as a result of renewed interest in the classical literature of paganism. When Savonarola was not more than seven years old, Pope Pius II, endeavouring to restore the situation, had done his utmost to stir up a Crusade against the Turkish Infidel. The Papacy itself, however, was suffering from a decline, and was incapable even of reforming the Church, much less of standing out as the saviour of Europe.

Of these events and of this state of things Savonarola was completely conscious. He belonged to a family well known at Court and fully aware of all that went on in public life. Not that the interests of its men-folk were political. They had achieved fame as medical men, and it was fully expected that Savonarola would follow the family custom. However, he displayed an intense dislike of a doctor's life, and his determination to find happiness and usefulness for himself in a different sphere was confirmed, when at the age of nineteen he had an unfortunate love affair and the girl on whom he had set his heart refused to marry him. For four years he lingered on awaiting divine direction, but a powerful sermon finally decided him, and at the age of twenty-three he offered himself as a postulant to the Dominican friars.

He had already shown marked ability in his studies and he was set to do teaching work, although he had asked to be given the more menial tasks. Later he was sent out to preach, but this he did only with indifferent success, until an address before the Provincial chapter attracted the notice of a friend of the great Lorenzo de Medici, who, when he heard of it, invited him to take up

F

his residence in his own town of Florence. Savonarola entered the Convent of St. Mark's, Florence, at the age of twenty-nine, and there he spent the remainder of his life.

It was some time even now before he found himself as a preacher. He was unwilling to employ that over-polished and rhetorical style of oratory which was popular at the moment. However, his burning enthusiasm, his obvious goodness, and his downright sincerity soon began to attract hearers. The Prophets and the Book of Revelation were his favourite subjects and they suited both his thought and his manner. He felt it his duty to preach the certainty of God's wrath against His rebellious children. He had no doubt that he was vouch-safed special visions to reinforce his lessons. Like Jeremiah before him, he felt no jubilation at this token of Divine favour, but was often deeply depressed by the doom he had to pronounce. If he had followed his own wish he would often have remained silent, but, as he was accustomed to say, 'an inward fire consumes my bones and compels me to speak.' As in the case of the Old Testament prophets, most of his revelations were concerned with the logical results of breaking moral laws. But his insight was such that even when he descended to details, his prophecies were generally fulfilled. This, of course, increased his reputation with the multitude and strongly reinforced his own certainty that he was specially guided by God.

It is in this respect that Savonarola appears before us as a genuine reformer. His prophetic preaching was directed against moral abuses. To us it is almost inconceivable that any so-called Christian society could be so corrupt as was Florence at that epoch. In the Italy

of his day, the church services were strongly maintained
and the formal purity of doctrine was stoutly defended;
yet in the lives of the more cultured classes, essential
Christianity had been replaced by an actual paganism.
It was the considered policy of the papacy during that
period to put itself at the head of the Renaissance movement in art and culture—a by no means unworthy
purpose. But in doing so, it had allowed its own moral
fibre to be utterly corrupted by a pagan manner of life.
If Alexander VI could give a public dinner to the prosti-
tutes of Rome, it was partly because public opinion had
already tolerated the recognition of Plato as a Christian
Saint, and the employment of a well-known courtesan
as an artist's model of the Blessed Virgin.

It was against all this kind of thing that Savonarola
stirred up the Florentines. Here at any rate, in this one
city, he would educate a public that would live in the
spirit of the Bible and would make no truce with the new
spirit of the Renaissance.

It was not that Savonarola failed to appreciate the
value of art and learning. His own Convent provided
the first public library in the whole of Italy. He was
himself a philosophical student of no mean order, and
as far as art was concerned, Botticelli was his friend
and illustrated some of his books; Michael Angelo was
one of his most constant hearers, and all the Della Robbia
were devoted to him. It is clear, then, that he was not
against art or learning, but only against the pagan and
licentious spirit with which they had become imbued.

These views of his he was able to act upon more completely when at the age of thirty-nine he became Prior
of his Convent and Provincial of his Order. He now had
behind him a solid body of disciples and he set to work to
reform the life and manners of the whole city.

The most spectacular point of attack was the annual Carnival with its procession, giving rise not only to vast expenditure of money, but also to much rough horse-play and a great deal of immorality. His method of dealing with this was to enlist the help of the children. He persuaded them to abandon their old method of holding up the citizens and demanding money for their own purposes, and to replace it by a street collection for the poor and needy. The children seem to have been just as pleased with the one diversion as the other, and certainly it contributed more to the general happiness of the people.

For at least two years, he induced the adult population to take an even more striking step. Instead of the usual Carnival Procession, they organized a parade to the central square of the city. There they found a huge bonfire on which they threw the more indecent and undesirable specimens of contemporary art and literature. This is the famous 'Burning of the Vanities,' which created so astonished an interest throughout the civilized world of the time.

Some of his contemporaries and some modern historians have denounced this practice on the ground that many of the things destroyed were priceless works of Art. Owing to the extreme volatility of the Italians of that period, it is possible that some of them at the height of their passion did destroy things, the loss of which was afterwards regretted; but in view of what we have already said about Savonarola's interest in art and artists, it is extremely unlikely that anything of real value was destroyed with his consent. In any case it is certain that far more good than harm was done by this wholesale burning. At a time when the connection between morality and religion was in danger of being lost, he recalled men and women to a recognition of the fact that God's own nature was moral goodness, and that without striving after such goodness, no one could hope to see His Face.

In the meantime, great changes had taken place in the political structure of Florence. Lorenzo de Medici had died, and been succeeded by the less able Piero de Medici. His reign came to an end when the French King, Charles VIII, was attacking Florence. It was found that Piero had handed over some of the city's fortresses to the enemy. There was a revolt and it looked as if there might be much bloodshed. The revolutionaries, however, attended Savonarola's preaching and his influence was such that a change of government took place without any forfeiture of life and without any excesses being committed.

The city then had to make the best terms it could with King Charles. When other ambassadors had failed, it was Savonarola who visited the King and so impressed him that the city was spared the horrors that usually accompanied the entry of a foreign army.

The words with which the friar addressed the King on this occasion have been preserved:

O most Christian king, thou art an instrument in the hand of the Lord, who sendeth thee to relieve the woes of Italy, as for many years I have foretold: and He sendeth thee to reform the Church which now lieth prostrate in the dust. But if thou be not just and merciful; if thou shouldest fail to respect the city of Florence, its women, its citizens, and its liberty; if thou shouldest forget the task the Lord hath sent thee to perform, then will He choose another to fulfil it; His hand shall smite thee, and chastise thee with terrible scourges. These things say I unto thee in the name of the Lord.

In the reconstruction of the city's government,

Savonarola played a leading role. In virtue of his position he was compelled, however unwillingly, to play the part of political adviser. The great Council which became the parliament of the State was most probably of his devising.

But more important than the actual ordering of the Government was the formation of a united civic spirit which made Florence the nursery of the best political minds of the next generation. As Lord Acton said, 'Savonarola believed that the way to make men better was to make them free.'

But it is not to be imagined that Savonarola could do all this without arousing against himself powerful enemies. Naturally, there were many in the city who would not appreciate the loss of the old gaiety and licentiousness. There were others who would resent the part he had played in getting rid of the tyranny of the Medici. But worst of all, by his denunciation of abuses in the Church, he had aroused against him the anger of the Papacy. Alexander VI was the worst Pope that ever sat on the throne of St. Peter. But he was an able man, and he may have thought that Florence under Savonarola was a threat to that unity of Italy which he was trying to bring about. In any case, he seems carefully to have nourished a quarrel with the Prior of the Dominican Convent and he finally excommunicated him.

From the point of view of ecclesiastical discipline, Savonarola made his position worse by ignoring the sentence. It gave his enemies within the city a handle against him, and when the Pope threatened to put the city under an interdict, the authorities begged him to cease his preaching. Not satisfied with this, his enemies tried to discredit him further. There was a ridiculous interlude when some Franciscans challenged the Dominicans to an ordeal by fire. All arrangements were made, but while the parties were disputing about the precise conditions of the test, rain came down and extinguished the fire. As was expected, the baffled crowd expended its resentment on Savonarola. Later there was an attack on the Monastery organized by the City Fathers themselves. Savonarola and two of his closest friends were taken and repeatedly put to torture. It is surprising that opinion, even in his own city, could so quickly have turned against him. Finally, Savonarola and his confederates were condemned to death. With two others he was taken out to the central square of the city and first hanged and then burnt.

Savonarola died, but his influence did not die. His example was remembered in the following century and inspired some of the best efforts and aspirations of that chequered time. But the lesson stands for all time and not least for this in which we are battling once again for that freedom which was his great political principle. But what of that other principle of moral goodness which in his eyes was even more important? Are we battling for that too? It is very necessary that we should make up our minds—'Are your minds set upon righteousness? . . .' The one cannot survive long without the other. Freedom is not licence, but it may easily degenerate into licence and then it is lost. We need both together: goodness in the moral sphere, freedom in the political. And the price of freedom is eternal vigilance—vigilance not only over the seas but over the stormy passions of our human hearts. Savonarola believed, according to Lord Acton, that 'The way to make men better is to make them free.' We might with more truth put it the other way round and say, 'The way to free men is to make them better.'

9

SIR THOMAS MORE, SAINTLY LAWYER

I WANT to paint for you the portrait of one who belonged to the transitional period between the Middle Ages and our modern world. This is Sir Thomas More, famous as the author of *Utopia*, and venerated by many as a Saint and Martyr.

He was born in 1478, the son of a Judge of the King's Bench. He was a regular Londoner, spending his early years in Cheapside, and his schooldays at a free school belonging to St. Anthony's Hospital in Threadneedle Street, on a site now occupied by the Bank of England.

He did not go on to one of the great Public Schools, although Eton and Winchester had then been founded, but at about the age of twelve he was placed in the family of the Archbishop of Canterbury, John Morton. The Archbishop was himself an able and well-educated man, of a deeply spiritual piety. The young boy received in his household an excellent training, which fitted him well for the great part he was afterwards to play in both the religious and the secular life of England.

At the age of fourteen he went up to Oxford, becoming a student at Canterbury College, an academy of learning which has now developed into the great institution of Christ Church with the Cathedral as its College chapel.

The Oxford of that day was beginning to open its doors to the new learning. The Renaissance which had already been put in train through the revival of interest in Greek language and literature, had received an additional fillip from the refugee scholars after Constantinople had been taken by the Turks in 1453. In Italy this Renaissance had taken the form of a return to the old Pagan humanism, with its love of the Fine Arts and literature, and its somewhat reckless *joie de vivre*.

In its passage to the North the revival had taken a more serious turn. The new interest in Greek had opened the way to a fresh understanding of the New Testament, and indeed to a new view of the whole meaning and character of the Christian religion. What this development portended was naturally not as clear in those days as to us; although we can hardly flatter ourselves that even now we have completely worked out its implications. Nevertheless it was a thrilling epoch. The adventures in the new world of thought were as romantic as the adventures overseas, which had resulted in the discovery of a new material world in America. People were already calling it the New Age.

More eagerly availed himself of the opportunities Oxford afforded for entering this new life of the mind and the spirit. Young as he was, he showed very great aptitude for scholarship, and he already began to reveal that individual genius which is a more priceless gift than any scholarship. Later that genius was to form for itself an appropriate environment in the friendship of two other notable men, who were also the spiritual children of the Renaissance—Colet and Erasmus.

John Colet was an Englishman who, after his Oxford career, travelled in Italy, acquired a considerable knowledge of Greek, and on his return lectured on the Pauline Epistles. He became Dean of St. Paul's, and was the founder of the famous London school of St. Paul's. Colet's aim was 'to bring back the Christianity of the Apostles and to clear away the thorns and briars with which it was overgrown.' That was the verdict of More's other friend, Erasmus. He was a Dutchman, of no fixed abode, who was attracted to England by an offer of freedom of thought, and by a pension which was granted to him through the kindness of Archbishop Warham. Without the exalted moral earnestness of Colet, he had even greater intellectual gifts. He levelled his wit against the obscurantism of the old-fashioned clergy and scholars, and set himself to reduce the necessary Articles of Faith to the fewest and simplest.

I have no time now to speak of the scholarly work performed by Erasmus, of his edition of the Greek Testament with the new Latin translation, representing as it does the first-fruits of Biblical Criticism, and laying down for all time the proper method, namely the comparison of manuscripts, for the finding of the true text; nor can I speak of his schemes for reforming the Church from within. But his own judgement upon himself may be quoted: 'My work has been to restore a buried literature and to recall Divines from their hair-splittings to a knowledge of the New Testament.'

But this is to anticipate. I do it in order to make clear the mental environment of More, and to place him against his proper background.

He did not stay at Oxford long. He came down, in fact, without taking his degree; probably because his father was afraid that the new learning might be too much for him and spoil him for his future career. He was marked out for the Law, and when he left Oxford he became a law student at New Inn, later transferring his allegiance to Lincoln's Inn. For a time he lived with his parents, but he later became a boarder in the Charterhouse Monastery, where he lived for four years.

It is probable that for a time he thought that his own

vocation might be to the monastic life. But in the end
it became clear to him that he was not cut out for such a
career, and in this conclusion Dean Colet, who was now
his spiritual adviser, concurred. Erasmus afterwards
said that the one thing that prevented More from giving
himself to that kind of life was that he could not shake off
his desire for the married state.

He did indeed marry, but not until two years after he
left the monastery. And that marriage reveals in him
a curious delicacy of mind which some may regard as
altogether too quixotic. His choice lay between the three
daughters of the Colt family.

Albeit his mind most served him to the second daughter, for
that he thought her the fairest and best favoured, yet when he
considered that it would be great grief and some shame also
to the eldest to see her younger sister preferred before her in
marriage, he then, of a certain pity, framed his fancy toward
her and soon after married her.

By this time he had formed a friendship with Erasmus,
had been called to the Bar, had delved into the study
of Greek, and had become a Member of Parliament.
Gradually he became a person of some reputation, and
on the occasion of the accession of Henry VIII he composed the Coronation Verses.

In 1511 he was appointed Reader at Lincoln's Inn.
The same year his wife died, and within a month he
married again. He had been engaged in literary labours.
He had published an amusing story of a Sergeant who
disguised himself as a friar. He had lectured on St.
Augustine's *City of God*, and he had translated the life of
Pico della Mirandola, one of the great figures of the
Renaissance. Now he set himself to write a History of
King Richard III, which marks an epoch in English
literature as establishing the biographical form which has

so often been imitated and is so extremely popular in our own day.

In 1515 he was a member of a political mission to Flanders. While there he continued the writing of his most famous book, *Utopia*, which he had begun some time before. Into this he was able to pour not only his literary skill, but all the wealth of his vivid imagination and his political and philosophical criticism.

It is a question how far we are to regard this work as a serious picture of More's ideal State, and how far it is to be regarded rather as an attempt to set people thinking about the grave questions of social life. He anticipated many of the questions which were to be seriously debated in later days. Sometimes indeed he is surprisingly modern. Thus he adumbrated not only the marriage of priests, but also a priesthood of women. Divorce appears to be allowed even for such a cause as incompatibility of temper. Euthanasia is practised; but war is regarded as something fit only for beasts. It is noteworthy that in Utopia provision is made for municipal hospitals, sanitary reform is encouraged, capital punishment is strictly limited, provision is made for old age, and the hours of labour are greatly reduced.

The work at once took its place as a masterpiece of European thought. It raised its author to a foremost place amongst the leaders of his age, and it was the first prose contribution that England, in her awakened scholarship, made to the development of European culture.

More's rising fame brought him to the notice of the young King, Henry VIII, who made him his secretary and took him among his attendants to the Field of the Cloth of Gold. In 1523 he was elected Speaker of the House of Commons, and honours began to pour thickly upon him, until in 1529 he became Lord Chancellor, the first commoner in the whole of English history to occupy that exalted position.

He was not to rest long upon this summit of prosperity. Henry VIII, in his effort to obtain an heir to his throne, had tried to get his first marriage declared null and void, and his second legalized. This had led to his quarrel with the Pope and his determination to throw off Papal dominance. The Clergy were induced to acknowledge him as 'supreme head of the Church, so far as God's law permits,' and the great lay officers of the Crown were expected to acquiesce in this position. More found it impossible and with rare honesty resigned the Lord Chancellorship in 1532.

In his misfortune the excellence of his character shone out more clearly than ever. His enemies did everything possible to prove that he had been guilty of the usual practices of men in high office. But in spite of all their efforts they could not find him guilty of having taken a single bribe. He had indeed been so circumspect that he had not even accepted a present in kind. He had amassed no fortune. His gifts to charity had been so extensive that he had saved practically nothing out of the considerable income that he had received. He bore his straitened circumstances with good humour, and said that as he had lived on little enough when he was an undergraduate at Oxford and a student in the Inns of Court, he could easily do the same again.

His misfortunes deepened. He was required to take the Oath of the King's Supremacy, but refused, and was thereupon committed to the Tower. Every effort was made to trap him into some admission which would make it possible to arraign him on a more serious charge. He was aware of the danger, and with legal skill refrained from committing himself. But he had little doubt of the issue.

His sorest trial lay in the fact that the members of his own family did their utmost to persuade him to yield. His wife accepted the greatest deprivations for herself in order that she might supply him with food. Nevertheless, being a woman, she could not help upbraiding him for a stubbornness she could not understand.

I marvel [she said] that you, that have been always hitherto taken for so wise a man, will now so play the fool to lie here in this close filthy prison, and be content thus to be shut up among mice and rats, when you might be abroad at your liberty, and with the favour and good will, both of the King and his council if you would but do as all the bishops and best learned of this realm have done. And seeing you have at Chelsea a right fair house, your library, your gallery, your garden, your orchard, and all other necessaries so handsome about you, where you might in the company of me, your wife, your children, and household, be merry. I muse what a God's name you mean here still thus fondly to tarry.

Even more difficult for him to bear was the long-drawn-out effort of his daughter Margaret to break down his seeming obstinacy, and so to secure his release. He found some ease of mind and recreation of spirit in writing a Dialogue of Comfort against Tribulation, a Treatise upon the Passion, and a little volume on receiving the Holy Communion.

In the end he was indicted for High Treason and a conviction was secured on what appears to have been the perjured evidence of one solitary individual. On his way back to the prison after his condemnation his daughter broke through the line of guards, ran up to him and flung herself about his neck, and the last lines he

ever wrote were inscribed on a scrap of paper with a piece
of coal to thank her and bid her farewell.

He had always had a reputation for a brightness and
vivacity amounting to actual merriness. As a boy he
was conspicuous for his gaiety, and it had been especially
noticed when he was a member of the household of
Cardinal Morton that he was a leader in the merry-
making at Christmas time. Erasmus commented on the
same trait.

His expression is pleasing and cordial, easily passing into a
smile, for he has the quickest sense of the ridiculous of any
man I ever met.

This gift lasted him even to the end, for, finding the
scaffold somewhat unfirm, he said to the officer who was
escorting him, 'I pray thee see me safely up, and for my
coming down let me shift for myself.'

It is this trait that I would like to leave in your
memories. The Roman Church has canonized Sir Thomas
More and officially enrolled him among the Saints.
Anglicans honour his memory as that of one of the three
great Oxford Reformers, Colet and Erasmus being the
other two. But all of us alike can reverence the name of
one who in the strength of his religion could face the
bitterest disappointment and even death itself with a
smile.

10

GEORGE HERBERT, PASTOR AND POET

THE candid speaker, even when he is discussing the lives of Saints, almost always finds some ground for criticism. It is often said that Saints are difficult people to live with, and it very seldom happens that we have to speak of one who has no faults at all. But such is my happy lot in speaking of George Herbert. I suppose that he must have possessed some defects of character, but if he did I do not know them. Our knowledge of him comes mostly from a very delightful sketch of his life, written by Izaac Walton, who is so famous in the history of English literature as the author of *The Compleat Angler*. That sketch, slight as it is, gives us the picture of an entirely lovable character.

In one respect Herbert was quite unlike those heroes of the Christian Faith whom I have recently discussed with you. He played a very small part on the great stage of public affairs. He might have played a leading role had he not decided to become a country parson.

The work that he did as Vicar of Bemerton occupied only three years, and the church in which he ministered (I know it well) is not as big as this private chapel from which I am speaking now.[1] But those few years lived in so humble a spot have left an indelible impression upon the whole life and character of the Church of England.

But let me go back to the beginning. George Herbert was of noble birth. His family name is that of the Earls

[1] Bishopsbourne, Brisbane.

of Pembroke, to whom he was closely related. His earliest home was Montgomery Castle in Wales. His father died when George was only four years old, leaving ten children—seven boys and three girls—which his mother used to describe as Job's number.

At the age of twelve he was sent to Westminster School, where he shewed considerable ability, and whence he obtained a scholarship to Trinity College, Cambridge. He took his degree at the age of eighteen, and received various appointments in the University until he was given the much-coveted post of Public Orator. As such it became his duty to write a letter of thanks to King James, when that monarch presented his book *Basilicon Doron*, or The Gift of the King, to the University. James was so pleased with the letter that he commented on it to the Earl of Pembroke, with whom he happened to be staying. The Earl said that he knew the writer very well, and that he was actually a kinsman. The King, smiling, asked 'that he might love him too, for he took him to be the jewel of the University.'

This auspicious introduction promised a brilliant career for the young man. He had to be frequently in attendance at Court, and he became a well-known figure in the scientific and literary circle with which the King was pleased to surround himself. Among his friends was Lord Bacon, who thought so much of his ability that he actually submitted his manuscripts for Herbert to read and criticize. Another friend was the learned and saintly Bishop Andrewes, and two other great Churchmen whom he knew well were Donne and Laud.

But his own path seemed to lie in the direction of diplomacy. He expected to receive high office of State, and in preparation for it he added to his classical attainments a knowledge of French, Spanish and Italian. But

G

presently his hopes were dashed by the death of the King and by that of two powerful friends who would have acted as his patrons.

We are reminded of St. Ignatius Loyola, who, finding his knightly career cut short by a desperate wound, pledged himself, as he lay wounded on the Field of Pampeluna, to become a Knight of God. However, Herbert's resolution was not taken so speedily. He retired into solitude for a period, and only after much conflict of mind determined to offer himself for ordination.

He was made deacon and was given a living. Finding his church in a bad state of repair, he immediately set to work to restore it. There was an amusing passage of arms with his mother over this task. He seems usually to have deferred to her advice. On this occasion, as he was already shewing signs of weak health she thought that such a task would be quite beyond his powers. 'George,' she said, 'it is not for your weak body and empty purse to undertake to build churches.' But he replied by expressing a hope that she 'would allow him, at the age of thirty-three, to become an undutiful son; for he had made a vow to God that, if he were able, he would rebuild that church.' He seems to have collected the money from his well-to-do friends and so to have got the work done.

His ideas on the subject of church furnishing are interesting. He took care that the reading pew and the pulpit should be separate and a little distant from each other. He was very particular to see that they should both be of an equal height, for, he said:

They should neither have a precedency or priority of the other; but that prayer and preaching, being equally useful, might agree like brethren, and have an equal honour and estimation.

Admission to the diaconate did not seem then the wholehearted step that it seems to-day. It was only after considerable hesitation that Herbert desired to go further. He decided both to become a priest and also to marry. Apparently he and the lady of his choice already knew a good deal of each other, although they had never actually met. But the proposal was made and accepted and they saw each other for the first time three days before marriage.

This was the somewhat unusual introduction to an idyllically happy married life. A home was found for them when Herbert was presented to the living of Bemerton, near Wilton, the seat of his relative the Earl of Pembroke. Izaak Walton describes a touching incident in connection with the ceremony of his induction:

When at his induction, we are told, he was shut into Bemerton Church, being left there alone to toll the bell (as the law requires him) he stayed so much longer than an ordinary time before he returned to those friends that stayed expecting him at the church-door, that his friend Mr. Woodnot looked in at the church-window, and saw him lie prostrate on the ground before the altar: at which time and place (as he after told Mr. Woodnot) he set some rules to himself, for the future manage of his own life; and then and there made a vow to labour to keep them.

Three days after, when he had changed his sword and silk clothes into a canonical habit, he went to meet his wife and saluted her in this somewhat quaint fashion:

You are now a minister's wife, and must now so far forget your father's house, as not to claim a precedence of any of your parishioners; for you are to know that a priest's wife can challenge no precedence or place but that which she purchases by her obliging humility.

It was on those lines that both of them set out to do their best in that little country parish near Salisbury.

The spirit that animated all his work can be judged by the book into which he poured all his thoughts on the priestly life, and which is still the guide of many of his successors in the priesthood. The book is generally known as *A Priest to the Temple*, but its sub-title is 'The Country Parson, His Character and Rule of Holy Life.'

In it he goes into every detail of the country parson's work, and he shews a shrewd knowledge of human character. One realizes how absorbing could be the task for any one who was prepared to give his whole soul to it. Here is no picture of a man falling into a machine-like routine, nor of one who is content if he fills a minimum round of petty duties, but of one whose whole life is concentrated upon his task and who regards everything as grist to his mill so long as it enables him to serve his people better.

Thus when he is discussing the subject of knowledge, he says, 'The country parson is full of all knowledge. They say it is an ill mason that refuseth any stone: and there is no knowledge, but, in a skilful hand, serves either positively as it is, or else to illustrate some other knowledge.'

Again we see how, like a good workman, he takes a real delight in his task. There is no foolish diffidence or shrinking. So, when he speaks of the parson in the pulpit, he says, boldly, 'The country parson preacheth constantly. The pulpit is his joy and his throne.' Very different from the 'coward's castle' that some people think it to be.

And not only the parson, but every member of his household is expected to live a life in accordance with his religious duties.

The country parson's wife [he says] is either religious, or night and day he is winning her to it. Instead of the qualities of the world, he requires only three of her: First a training of her children and maids in the fear of God, with prayers and catechizing, and all religious duties. Secondly, a curing and healing of all wounds and sores with her own hands; which skill either she brought with her or he takes care she shall learn it of some religious neighbour. Thirdly, a providing for her family in such sort that neither they want a competent sustentation, nor her husband be brought in debt.

It can be imagined that duties carried out in this spirit brought a ready response. The people in the neighbourhood were delighted to find that Mr. Herbert said the Daily Office in church at 'the canonical hours of ten and four.' Walton says that most of his parishioners and many gentlemen in the neighbourhood constantly made a part of his congregation twice a day.

And some of the meaner sort of his parish did so love and reverence Mr. Herbert, that they would let their plough rest when Mr. Herbert's Saints-bell rang to prayers, that they might also offer their devotions to God with him, and would then return back to their plough.

One recreation Herbert allowed himself. He was devoted to music. Even when he was at Cambridge he had found it a great solace. He would say that 'it did relieve his drooping spirits, compose his distracted thoughts and rest his weary soul so far above the earth that it gave him an earnest of the joys of heaven before he possessed them.' And now, finding himself so close to Salisbury, he was able to go into the Cathedral Church twice every week to listen to the service. When the service was over he would join a little private party in the Close, where there would be more music, and he himself would sing to the lute or the viol hymns and anthems which he himself had composed.

There is a story that once that polite society of gentle-men musicians was shocked to see the usually spruce Mr. Herbert arrive in a very dirty, mud-stained condition. When he noticed their surprise he told them how he had met a poor man with a still poorer horse that had fallen down under its load. They were both in such distress that Herbert had taken off his canonical coat and had helped the poor man first to unload, and afterwards to load the animal again. This seemed a quite outrageous thing to such a gathering; but he told them that the thought of what he had done would prove music to him at mid-night, 'And now,' he added, 'let us tune our instruments.'

But Herbert was not to remain long in the enjoyment of these surroundings. He had apparently shewn signs of consumption for many years, and now the disease gained rapidly upon him, and within a short time the end had come. But before he died he had sent to his friend Nicholas Ferrar the manuscript of another book, which shewed how he had been wont to spend some of his solitude. This was a book of poems, which revealed more clearly than any biography the ardent conflicts of his soul.

With many of those poems we are familiar because they have found their way into our hymn books. But there are others which breathe a gentle piety unsurpassed by any sacred songs in the language. Such a one is the poem on Lent beginning,

> Welcome, dear feast of Lent: who loves not thee,
> He loves not temperance or authority,
> But is composed of passion.
> The Scriptures bid us fast; the Church says, now:
> Give to thy mother what thou wouldst allow to
> To every corporation.

There is another, called 'The Pulley,' which will awake an echo in every truly religious heart.

The Pulley

When God at first made man,
Having a glass of blessing standing by;
Let us (said He) pour on him all we can;
Let the world's riches, which dispersed lie,
    Contract into a span.

So strength first made a way;
Then beauty flow'd, then wisdom, honour, pleasure:
When almost all was out, God made a stay,
Perceiving that, alone of all His treasure,
    Rest in the bottom lay.

For if I should (said He)
Bestow this jewel also on My creature,
He would adore My gifts instead of Me,
And rest in nature, not the God of nature:
    So both should losers be.

Yet let him keep the rest,
But keep them with repining restlessness:
Let him be rich and weary, that at least,
If goodness lead him not, yet weariness
    May toss him to My breast.

But I must not go on quoting. I should only like to impress upon your minds a picture of this gracious seventeenth-century figure, one of the most typical representatives of English piety. When we allow for the peculiar phraseology of the time, which savours to us a little of priggishness, we are left with the remembrance of one who endeared to him all that knew him whether of high or low degree, and who maintained with undiminished cheerfulness in spite of long and gradually deepening weakness his unremitting toil for God and human souls.

11

NICHOLAS FERRAR, CONTEMPLATIVE

I AM going to choose for the next of my saints and leaders of the Christian Church a Contemplative, a man who deliberately retired from the world in order to give himself up entirely to the things which concern God and the soul. We have already had a monk and friar to consider, but the interesting thing about them was that in spite of their profession they were compelled to lead active lives. In this case the process is reversed, and we have a man who was exceedingly successful in the active life retiring from it in order to live as a recluse.

The hero in question is Nicholas Ferrar, who flourished in the time of Charles I. His portrait reminds us very much of the pictures of Charles I—the pointed beard and moustache, the hair long and brushed straight back from the forehead but curling into the neck, the big but heavily-lidded eyes, the white ruff fitting closely to the neck, the tight-buttoned coat with wide over-sleeves, the inner sleeves fastened close to the wrist with white lawn cuffs.

The fortunes of the King are to some extent paralleled in those of Ferrar and his family. We shall be dealing with a period which combines romantic and tragic circumstances. In the midst of them Nicholas Ferrar stands as one who kept the torch of contemplative religion alight at a time when such ideals might easily have been quenched.

Nicholas was born in 1593, the fourth of the seven sons

of a great merchant adventurer. Nicholas Ferrar the father was a close friend and ally of those great sea-dogs Drake, Frobisher and Hawkins, with whom he was associated at the business end of a number of hazardous enterprises.

The younger Nicholas was a particularly bright boy, the foremost scholar at his school, going up to the University of Cambridge at what we should consider the ridiculously early age of thirteen. He shewed an amazing progress there and soon after taking his degree was elected a Fellow of his College with a view to reading medicine.

He spent seven years altogether in the University, and then his health gave cause for great anxiety and he was advised to travel on the Continent. He went in the company of the Princess Elizabeth, daughter of James I; but he left her train soon after his arrival on the Continent, and then he travelled everywhere alone from Holland and round most of Europe down to Spain.

He had sundry adventures during that time, once nearly dying of fever at Marseilles. But an escape which left a deeper impression upon him was on a narrow road in the Italian mountains. There was barely enough room for a single horseman between the rock on the one side and the yawning precipice on the other. As he rode along he suddenly saw to his horror a donkey charging down towards him with a big baulk of timber lying at right angles across its back, thus occupying the whole space of the narrow path. It seemed that nothing could save the traveller, when suddenly the donkey stumbled, the log of timber swung round lengthwise from head to tail, and the animal passed by leaving Nicholas unharmed. It turned out that the donkey had escaped from a timber merchant higher up the mountain, who had been loading a team but had not succeeded in fastening this particular log securely before the animal broke away.

Such events as these gave the young man an even more serious turn of mind than would be accounted for by the natural self-reliance acquired on his long and lonely travels. Returning to England towards the end of 1618, with his health restored, he intended to take up his Fellowship at Cambridge; but unfortunately his father's affairs had become involved and he decided to stay in London to help him put things straight.

The Ferrars were much concerned in the Virginia Company, which had been formed for the purpose of establishing a colony in that part of America visited by Sir Walter Raleigh and named by him Virginia after the virgin queen Elizabeth. For six years Nicholas worked hard at the affairs of the Company and was actually appointed its Deputy Governor—no small compliment to a man who was barely thirty.

His ability became known and he was much sought after, being offered a Professorship in mathematics. This he refused out of modesty, and also perhaps because he foresaw the fresh difficulties that were likely to descend upon the Virginia Company. The Spanish party at Court was very anxious to get the government of the Colony out of English hands; and they actually succeeded in having the charter withdrawn. This, of course, was something very like treachery. Nicholas put up for Parliament, got himself elected, and then took the lead in impeaching the man who was mostly responsible for the dissolution of the Company, no less a person than the Lord Treasurer of the day, the Earl of Middlesex. So successful was Ferrar's attack upon him that he was convicted by the Peers of bribery and corruption, fined the enormous sum of £50,000 and declared incapable of sitting in Parliament.

This, of course, put Ferrar in the very forefront of the public life of the day, and he gained such a reputation that it would have been natural for him to pursue a public career. But this one taste of political life, although he had been so successful in it, more than sufficed. He determined to leave the public arena as soon as he could, and to make an experiment in the way of restoring in the English Church the life of religion in a community.

It was eighty years or so since Henry VIII had dissolved the English monasteries, but Nicholas had no doubt seen something of monastic life in his travels on the Continent. However, he wanted to return to an earlier form of monasticism than was characteristic of any of the medieval types. At the beginning of the movement in the fourth century Christians had been accustomed to live an ascetic life in their own homes. That was the source from which all Christian monasticism flowed, and Nicholas thought it might be repeated in his own case.

There have not been many Christian leaders in the course of history who have been able to change the lives of their own families and to win their own relatives to share in the special effort after a higher degree of holiness. Bernard of Clairvaux did it when he led his male relatives to share with him the austerities of the Cistercian Order. But Ferrar was unique in that he was able to carry with him in his endeavour both the male and female members of his family together with the children of all ages.

The plague was raging in London, and his mother, now a widow, had bought a practically deserted property in Huntingdonshire known as Little Gidding. It consisted of a big mansion, with a church and with a cottage for the shepherds, and a considerable amount of land given up entirely to pasturage. Nicholas sent his mother down to this property to get her away from the plague, and it was there that he decided, with her enthusiastic support, to start the religious community which was to become famous as 'The Protestant Nunnery.'

It was an extraordinary venture. You would think that nobody in his senses could expect to manage a community of no fewer than forty souls, all living in close contact with each other, consisting of members of three generations, and including not only blood relations but in-laws as well.

The children were in some respects the most important members of the community. At any rate the household was very largely organized around them. Three school-masters were kept and the children from the surrounding villages were invited to come and join in their lessons.

As one might expect, there was occasional trouble. Nicholas had an elder brother, John, whose wife was not nearly so ready to fall under Nicholas' influence as her husband. The worst quarrel arose when she accused Nicholas of having gone behind her back and forced her small boy into breeches earlier than she desired. This was apparently the culmination of a number of com-plaints. Nicholas carefully wrote out a letter in which he denied having influenced her husband in any way, and then he called them both in before him, and read out the letter which contained not only this denial, but also a moving exhortation to the lady to yield herself to the undoubted love and affection of her husband. She, how-ever, we are told, flounced out of the room and refused to accept the explanation.

How much of this kind of thing there was we do not know, because the life of Nicholas was written by his brother John who regarded him as a complete saint and makes no mention of any such untoward incidents. Such intimate touches we only know from family letters which are just beginning to be published to the world. However, I think there was really very little trouble: indeed, miraculously little, in view of the curiously assorted company which inhabited this Manor House at Little Gidding.

The whole household was strictly ordered on monastic lines. Religious exercises at home and services in the church took up a large part of the day. The children joined in most of them and learned great passages of Scripture which they recited with much unction. A big dovecote or pigeon-house was made into a schoolroom, where the education seems to have been on very sound lines. Nicholas was human enough to realize that work and devotions were not sufficient for children, and he arranged that their time-table should include opportunities for archery and such pastimes as running and vaulting. Music also was greatly encouraged and there was more than one organ in the house.

The older girls were brought up in domestic ways and took it in turns, a month at a time, to do the house-keeping—no light task, because in addition to the forty inmates of the house there were always a lot of children from the neighbourhood who came in to recite psalms and to share the midday repast on Sundays. And once the place became known there was a constant stream of visitors of high and low degree who had to be given some light refreshment, although it was the rule of the household not to ask them to stay to a proper meal or to remain for the night.

One of the pleasant recreations of the community was to write and act plays of religious interest. Another was to read stories that were likely to have a moral as well as an

aesthetic value. You might be interested if I quoted a
sample story such as was read by one of the young people
during meal times. The point of this story is to shew
that the contemplative and the active life do best when
they are taken together and not in separation. The story
is as follows:

Certain Strangers, going to an holy Man of great fame,
told him, that, having heard of the great Grace of God which
was in him, they were come to receive Edification by his
Doctrine and Example; professing themselves to be, as he
was, despisers of all worldly Things for the Sake of heavenly.

The old Man, being then busie in making of wicker baskets,
comanded his Disciple who waited on him, to bring out
Rods and Tools, saying unto them, Brethren, we will do two
good Things together, work and praise God.

They answered, they did not use to work. Not work,
replied the old Man, half amazed! What do you then, said
he, and how do you serve God? We spend the time together,
answered they, in Prayer, according to the Apostle's Command,
Pray without ceasing. (1 *Thess*. v. 17.)

The old Man paused awhile in deep Contemplation; at
last, lifting up his Head, he asked them, do you eat at all?
They answered, yes. And who then prays for you, said he?
They not knowing what to answer, he doubled his Demand,
do you ever sleep? They answered, yes. And who then prays
for ye, continued he? They, seeming confounded, the old
Man, with great Gravity and Meekness said unto them, You
see you do not what you profess, *pray without ceasing*; but are
Transgressors of that very Precept which you pretend most
to observe. But I will tell you how much better I perform it
than you. In the Morning, and seven Times a day, I offer
Prayer and Praises to God. The rest of the Time I bestow in
laborious Works, such as you see; and out of the Profit which
I get thereby, I first take what sufficeth for my own Main-
tenance, & then bestow the rest upon the Poor; who therefore
(blessing God for the Comfort which they receive by my

Means) pray for me both when I eat and when I sleep. And thus, I either by myself, or other always *pray without ceasing*.

The spiritual exercises were maintained throughout the night as well as the day, several of the men sharing the duty of keeping the night watches. Nicholas himself was always aroused at one o'clock in the night, and does not seem to have gone back to bed again, while for the rest of the household the day began at four o'clock in summer and five o'clock in winter.

The task on which they were most commonly engaged was that of compiling harmonies of the Gospels. Although these were done on the scissors-and-paste method it was with such care that it was impossible to tell without careful inspection that they were not printed straight out in the ordinary manner. A lady who was a professional bookbinder was invited to the house and kept there until she had taught all her skill to the members of the household, and the most beautiful examples of book-binding of that period proceeded from Little Gidding. Some of them are museum pieces in England to-day.

It was these books that especially interested King Charles I. It is related that a Harmony of the Gospels, made and bound by two of the young ladies, was presented by them to the King, who spent a few hours at Little Gidding in 1633 on his way to Scotland.

The King's interest in the establishment no doubt helped to call a certain amount of undesirable attention to the place, and it incurred the suspicion of the Puritan party. There seems to have been no active unpleasantness so long as Nicholas was alive. But he died in 1637. The Community had by this time begun to grow smaller. The old lady, Mrs. Ferrar, had died three years before; and one of the nieces, who had, with her elder sister, vowed herself to perpetual virginity, died a year after

Nicholas. Several of the other nieces married and went away, and the nephews had already gone to take up various professions.

As the King's unpopularity deepened, opportunity was found to attack the Gidding community. In 1641 these gentle people, whose lives were given up to the service of God and the exercise of charity among their neighbours, were made the subject of a discreditable lampoon in a pamphlet addressed to Parliament entitled *The Arminian Nunnery.*

The next year, six months before the outbreak of Civil War, the King paid a second visit to Little Gidding, accompanied by the Princes Charles and Rupert. We are told that the King on that occasion gave to four widows, who were maintained at the cost of the establishment in a separate part of the house, five pieces of gold which he had won the night before at cards, asking them to pray for him. The young nobles in the meantime had made a happy raid on the buttery and found some excellent apple pie which they tried in vain to induce the King to share with them.

Once again Charles was at Little Gidding in May 1646, when he was fleeing from Oxford to hand himself over to the Scottish army. John Ferrar, the elder brother, who was now in charge, received His Majesty with all possible duty and respect, but only hid him for a few hours; after which he thought it wise to take him through the dark night to a more remote hiding-place where he was less likely to be discovered.

This brought disaster on the Community. The Parliamentary soldiers came and rifled the place. The inmates happily had had warning and escaped betimes. The buildings, particularly the church, with its ornaments, received the full fury of the iconoclasts. The lectern was thrown into a neighbouring pond, the organ was broken up and set on fire, and some of the sheep were roasted over it. Many of the books and manuscripts were destroyed and the more valuable of the plate and furniture was taken off.

Thus terminated the effort so carefully inaugurated by Nicholas Ferrar to establish in at least one spot in England a community which could be wholly given over to spiritual interests. As we look back upon his brief enjoyment of the retired life and upon the destruction in which the place was involved, we might wonder whether it was all worthwhile. The answer should be sought not only in the monastic fortunes of the older members of the Community but also in the influence received by many young people, an influence that was to last throughout their own careers and be handed on through them to future generations.

But there are broader considerations than this. The experiment so nobly made and so consistently carried through by Nicholas Ferrar preserved in England the flame of a religious ideal, which was indeed dimmed for a century or two afterwards, but which burned up brightly again in later years and has resulted in a number of religious communities which have spread their beneficent influence around the world.

Not only so, but by this effort of Nicholas Ferrar there was stored up in dark and materialistic days the memory of a pure and undefiled religion which consisted in visiting the fatherless and widow in their affliction and in keeping oneself unspotted from the world. That ideal can never entirely die out so long as there are some individuals who are prepared to give themselves wholly to it. And of such individuals Nicholas Ferrar was a conspicuous example.

H

12

DR. JOHNSON, DEVOUT WIT AND CRITIC

IT is often debated whether the clergyman or the layman has the better opportunity of exercising an influence for good. The clergyman, of course, has the greater number of contacts and has the pulpit for his platform, but his efforts are discounted by their professional character. The layman, on the other hand, mixes more intimately with the indifferent and the actually antagonistic, but his efforts in a religious direction are often rejected, precisely because he is not a professional, and is therefore alleged to be guilty of trespassing upon ground which does not properly belong to him. Whatever answer may be given to this question in general, there can be little doubt that during the eighteenth century it was a layman who set the tone for the society, especially the intellectual society, of his day. Not Bishop Butler, nor even John Wesley, exercised the widest influence, but that stout Anglican layman, Samuel Johnson.

It was the period when Christianity was striving hard to maintain itself against an agnostic philosophy. It was the period of Voltaire and of the Enlightenment. Typical people of the age felt that in order to safeguard the frail bark of religion in the stormy seas that buffeted her it was necessary to jettison all the superfluous cargo of minute beliefs and even the tackle of specific dogmas, and to retain only the anchor of a hope in immortality and the rudder of a belief in the existence of God. Otherwise the ship of Faith could not be brought into port at all. Against that background Dr. Johnson stands out as the supporter of a full-blooded Christianity, a churchmanship of the genuine old High Church variety, going out to attack the enemy in his own seas, with all the guns blazing and with a contemptuous certainty of victory that often had already won him the battle before it was joined. He was a giant in the world of literature and morality, and the fact that he inspired both with intense religious feeling was perhaps the most significant feature in the conceptual history of the eighteenth century.

Johnson's early life was a story of continual struggle against misfortune. His father was a bookseller in Lichfield. As a child, the boy suffered from scrofula, which was a disease known as the 'King's evil,' because it was supposed to be curable by the touch of a reigning monarch. For this remedy, he was taken to London, and Queen Anne touched him, the last occasion on which we read of the application of this supposed cure. Actually, it was not very effective in Johnson's case, as he was a sufferer all his life from the results of the disease, being to some extent disfigured, near-sighted, and hard of hearing to the end of his days.

In spite of the poor family fortune, enough money was scraped together, partly through the interest of friends, to send him to Pembroke College, Oxford. There he was for a time a somewhat wild youth, although he was an intelligent one, having read widely in a desultory fashion before coming up to the University. But he was as candid with his tutors as he was afterwards with men who boasted of literary craftsmanship. On one occasion when his tutor fined him for not turning up at a lecture, Johnson replied, 'Sir, you have sconced me twopence for non-attendance at a lecture not worth a penny!' He never had much belief in lectures but was devoted to reading. At the University he followed his own later advice—'A man ought to read as his inclination leads him; what he reads as a task will do him little good. A young man should read five hours in a day, and so may acquire a great deal of knowledge.'

The failure of his father's business made it necessary for him to leave Oxford before taking a degree. He tried to help his father in the shop, but was so interested in the contents of the books, that he could not get on with the business of selling them. After this failure, he became an under-master in a school, but he did not make much of a success at this either. At the age of twenty-seven he made an extraordinary marriage with a widow of forty-eight whom nobody else could bear, but he was devoted to her all the rest of her life. She brought him a dowry of eight hundred pounds and with that they bought a school, but in eighteen months they received only three pupils and so were compelled to give it up. One of the pupils, however, was David Garrick, who later became the world's greatest actor.

With him Johnson proceeded to London in 1737. Garrick soon made good on the stage, but Johnson went through a period of hardship from which neither he nor his manners ever recovered. His friend of this period was Richard Savage, with whom, as Johnson afterwards said, whole nights were spent in conversation:

. . . not under the hospitable roof of a tavern, where warmth might have invigorated their spirits, and wine dispelled their care; but in a perambulation round the squares of Westminster, St. James's in particular; when all the money they could both raise was less than sufficient to purchase for them the shelter and sordid comforts of a night cellar.

Actually he removed to London at a very awkward time for one who wanted to make a living out of literature. The period when literary artists had put themselves under the patronage of some great person, who supported them, had now come to an end. On the other hand, the period when literature might look for its reward to sales among a considerable public had not yet begun. Johnson tried to solve the difficulty by doing occasional work for magazines. His most remunerative effort in this direction was a regular job of reporting parliamentary debates for the *Gentleman's Magazine*. Such reporting was contrary to the law and the debates had to be given under an assumed name as having taken place in the Senate of Liliput. Visitors, who were smuggled in by the influence of the publisher, brought Johnson notes, and on that basis he wrote up the speeches according to his imagination, taking care, as he said himself, 'that the Whig dogs did not get the better of the discussion.'

Perhaps the most famous speech was one that he put into the mouth of Pitt:

Sir, the atrocious crime of being a young man, which the honourable gentleman has with such spirit and decency charged upon me, I shall neither attempt to palliate or deny but content myself with wishing that I may be one of those whose follies may cease with their youth, and not of that number who are ignorant in spite of experience.

The tide of Johnson's fortunes began to turn when he was asked to be responsible for the compilation of an English Dictionary. He was offered £1,500 for the finished job, but he had to provide his own clerks and pay his own expenses out of that sum. It took him eight years to complete, but it brought him great fame, and made him at once the arbiter of English letters. Some of his definitions have become famous for their humour, as for instance ' *oats*, a grain, which in England is given to horses but in Scotland supports the population.'

It was now that his influence began to be felt in the moral as well as the literary sphere. This was to some extent the result of a magazine, called *The Rambler*, nearly the whole of which he wrote himself. When the magazine ceased publication and his essays were published in a collected form, the book ran through many editions and confirmed the public's admiration of Johnson as a majestic teacher of moral and religious wisdom.

It was at this time, however, that private grief overtook him in the death of his wife. The removal of her influence seems to have made him grow careless in his literary output, although he was always inclined to indolence. At any rate in 1756 he was imprisoned for a debt of £5 18*s*. 0*d*., an ignominious position from which he was delivered by one of his friends. About this time he was asked to consider the possibility of taking Holy Orders, but he decided that that was not his calling. It was a fortunate decision as the methodical discipline of the clerical life might easily have proved destructive of his genius and robbed him of those peculiar opportunities which as a layman he employed to the full. In consequence of this determination he still remained in poverty, and when his mother died in 1759, he had hurriedly to write a book in order to obtain sufficient money to pay for the expenses of her funeral.

Freedom from want at last came to Johnson in the shape of a Government pension of £300 a year. The offer of it put him in a rather awkward position. In his Dictionary he had defined 'pension' as pay given to a state hireling for treason to his country. The point was that Johnson was a strong Jacobite. How could he then favour those who received pensions from Hanoverian kings, and how could he himself after that luckless definition take a pension from George III? He exposed his scruples to Lord Bute, the minister through whom the grant was being made. Lord Bute assured him that it was given for work he had done in the past, but it would not fetter him in the least for the future. This did not save him from good-humoured chaff on the part of his friends, but he was ready for them with his usual wit and common sense: 'It is true that I cannot now curse the House of Hanover; nor would it be decent for me to drink King James' health in the wine that King George gives me money to pay for. But, Sir, I think that the pleasure of cursing the House of Hanover, and drinking King James' health, are amply over-balanced by three hundred pounds a year.'

In the following year Johnson's acquaintance was sought by Boswell, from whom the world was to learn so many intimate details about the life and conversation of the hero of Fleet Street. Opportunities for hearing his conversation became more frequent a year later when the Club was founded. The most noteworthy members of that Club were Sir Joshua Reynolds, the artist, Edmund Burke, the politician, Goldsmith, the author, Garrick, the actor, and Gibbon, the historian. In this society Johnson was at his best. Here opinions were expressed and tastes formulated which set the fashion throughout the whole country. It would be much more true to say of the Club, than of the Universities of the period, that 'what these people say to-day, the world thinks to-morrow.' In this select circle, Johnson was supreme, proving himself the Prince of English talkers as well as the most vivid and outstanding figure of its literary society.

Dublin was the first of our Universities to recognize his outstanding position and confer on him an honorary doctorate. It was not until ten years after that his own University of Oxford gave him a D.C.L. and he began to use the title of Doctor by which he has ever since been known.

Although he was attached to London, he frequently paid visits to Oxford and his home town, Lichfield, but in 1773 he went much farther afield and with Boswell undertook a journey to the Hebrides. Even there his extraordinary influence was felt, and it is said that as a result of his complaints about the bareness of the landscape, many of the Highland landowners began to plant the woods which now lend so much beauty to their country.

He was becoming an old man, but at the age of sixty-five he began to write his *Lives of the Poets*, a series which is still a standard authority for the poets of the period. For the declining years of his life he lived, if not in affluence, at any rate in sufficient ease. It might indeed be said that he lived in comfort, if it had not been that his generosity had led him to fill his house with an extraordinary company of old, ugly, blind and diseased people, who survived on his bounty and disturbed him with their continual quarrels and complaints. As one of his biographers recorded:

At the head of the household was an elderly blind and peevish lady named Williams. There was also another poor old woman, Mrs. Desmoulins and her daughter, and another destitute female, Polly Carmichael, whom her benefactor described briefly as 'a stupid slut.' On the male side there was Levett, an old and incompetent quack doctor, and Frank, a negro servant.

It could hardly be wondered that when such a society

filled his house, he found many opportunities of going out.
But he was careful not to offend the susceptibilities of his
protégés. Indeed his kindness was as great as his fame
and that was such, that when he died in 1784, no other
place than Westminster Abbey was found to be fitting
for his tomb.

It is to Boswell's *Life* that we owe our greatest
knowledge of Johnson's character. That *Life* has been
recognized as the greatest biography in the English
language. It is still the marvel of scholars that Boswell
could have written it. Macaulay made a paradoxical
statement that he could only do it because he was so
great a fool. But the absence of all reticence, which makes
Boswell seem foolish to some minds, was his greatest
qualification as a biographer. Scholastic opinion has
now come round to the view that Boswell was himself an
experienced literary artist. But to do his best work, a
great portrait painter requires a great subject, and here
we have both united.

To Johnson's contemporaries conversation was the
finest of the arts. However great a man might be as a
scholar or a writer, it was his conversation which alone
could place him in the front rank in the eyes of his
colleagues. That is precisely the standard of judgement
that Johnson applied to himself. Two things were
necessary for good conversation—knowledge and wit.
To these Johnson added a monumental common sense
which was the foe of all sham and humbug and of every
kind of sentimentalism. It was this common sense which
made his judgement sound and endeared him to the more
serious section of English society.

The evidences of his wit are piled up in paragraph
after paragraph of the *Life*. We can see how he watched

every opportunity to use it, and by the use of it clinched some argument or annihilated some opponent. But if his wit failed, he was not above using heavier means. Goldsmith complained of him, that if his pistol-shot failed to find its mark, he would hit you over the head with the butt-end of the weapon. But as a rule his gleeful enjoyment of victory lessened the blow for his opponent. We see Johnson after some such sally, lumbering up from his chair, crossing over to the fireplace, grunting, and gurgling and shouting with laughter.

But Goldsmith discovered the deeper side of his friend's character, and when he dedicated *She Stoops to Conquer* to him, wrote in the dedication:

It may serve the interest of mankind to inform them that the greatest wit may be found in a character without impairing the most unaffected piety.

Of Johnson's piety we have as much evidence as of his wit. He first became a definitely religious person when as an undergraduate at Oxford he read that splendid book, Law's *Serious Call*. Religion was to him no mere vague pietism but something definite and concrete to be expressed in everything that he thought and did. Amidst all the vague Deism of the time, he stood out as an intensely convinced Anglican. Boswell made a great mistake about that once. It was the time when the Convocations had been silenced by the Government and not allowed to conduct any business. Boswell told Johnson what absurd things people were saying about him in this connection. Even Hume, the philosopher, had avowed that Johnson had said that he would be ready to stand in front of a cannon, if only he could get Convocation restored to its proper function. To Boswell's intense surprise, Johnson not only admitted the truth of the statement, but asserted that he would indeed be willing to sacrifice his life for so splendid a cause. But these strongly held opinions did not prevent Johnson from being what nowadays is called 'broad-minded.' 'For my part,' he said, 'I think all Christians, whether Papist or Protestant, agree in the essential articles, and that their differences are trivial, and rather political than religious.'

Like every truly religious person, he had a deep sense of reverence. Seeing Boswell off at Harwich, when the latter was proceeding on a voyage to the Continent, Johnson bade him first kneel in the church and commend himself to his Creator and Redeemer. Again, the discernment of reverence in another assured from him a favourable judgement. 'Campbell,' he said, 'is a good man, a pious man. I am afraid that he has not been in the inside of a church for many years; but he never passes a church without pulling off his hat. This shows that he has good principles.'

It was probably this sense of reverence that he felt outraged by the thought of a woman preaching in church. A woman preaching, he said, was 'like a dog walking on its hind legs. It is not well done. The wonder is that it is done at all.' This sense of reverence deepened sometimes into a profound melancholy, and nowhere was it more obvious than in his thoughts of death. Boswell never came nearer to losing his friendship than he did on an unlucky occasion when he made the mistake of dealing lightly with the subject. This trait in Johnson's character is probably seen at its best in his attitude towards prayer. He would pray with his negro boy Francis, and help him to prepare for his Communion, and even when parting with his mother's maid who had been in her service for over forty years, he did not bid her good-bye without saying a short prayer with her. We still have the prayer that he composed before his last reception of Holy Communion:

Enforce and accept my imperfect repentance; make this commemoration available to the confirmation of my faith, the establishment of my hope, and the enlargement of my charity, and make the death of Thy Son Jesus Christ effectual to my redemption.

13

JOHN KEBLE, PASTOR AND SCHOLAR

THE Common Room at Oriel College, Oxford, looks to-day very much as it did in the early part of the nineteenth century when Keble, Pusey and Newman often gathered there together. Some of the portraits on the walls are new, but there is the same graceful Adam fireplace, the long oval polished table with its spindly legs, and the same demure straight-backed chairs. It was in these last that Cardinal Newman noticed a change when he revisited the College towards the end of his life. Red leather pads had been let into the backs to make them a little more comfortable, and Newman complained of the luxury into which the Fellows had fallen.

The remark was more than half serious, and it throws a flood of light on the character of the great religious Movement with which those three friends were associated. Particularly it illustrates the character of Keble, the strongest and staunchest of them all.

Those who think that the Oxford Movement had anything to do with the niceties of ecclesiasticism make a most egregious mistake. The keynote both of the Movement and of the character of those who inspired it was a desire for holiness. And that holiness was reflected according to the temper of the times in a profound austerity.

It was this austerity and this heartfelt cry for holiness that struck so strangely upon the ears of contemporary Englishmen. Both Church and State at that time were

afflicted by a deadly complacency which made any
desire for improvement impossible. English people had
recently seen something of the French Revolution, and
of the 'enthusiasm' that went along with it, and as far
as they were concerned they were content to stand in the
old ways and to congratulate themselves that they were
not as other men are.

In contrast with this spirit John Keble stands out
as a restorer of forgotten truth, and it is in that character
that I shall ask you to think of him. He was a
most lovable person, as you can see at once if you study
the beautiful portrait of him by Richmond which has
been so often reproduced. Certainly he was not born for
controversy. He was shy, diffident, often doubtful about
himself and his future, but capable of a bright and pleasing
gaiety which attracted to him not only his pupils but also
many who were his opponents. He himself confessed to a
real love for Thomas Arnold, who was very definitely on
the other side. The most brilliant of his friends, Hurrell
Froude, said of him, 'Keble is my fire, but I am his poker.'

But the austerity was there all the time. He once
heard Froude, in his light and easy way, say that he
thought William Law's *Serious Call* a 'clever book.' Keble
took him aside and rebuked him. 'It seems to me just
as if you had said that the Day of Judgement would be a
pretty sight.'

Keble belonged to an able family. His father, who was
a country parson, had been a Fellow of his College, and
his brother also enjoyed that honour. Keble himself
went up to the University very early and actually won
a double First at the age of eighteen. In those days the
Oriel Fellowships were given as the result of examination
and were regarded as the Blue Ribbon of scholarship.
Keble won his Fellowship at the age of nineteen, and in

the following year carried off no fewer than three University prizes. This does not imply that he was in any sense brilliant. He had none of the genius of Newman or Froude, but he was a painstaking and able scholar who could always be relied upon for solid achievement where his cleverer colleagues might either succeed beyond his capacities or fail altogether.

Having won his Fellowship he was ordained, and for some time occupied himself in parochial duties. Then at the age of twenty-six, in 1818, he was called back to Oriel to take up duties as tutor. He performed these duties in a most conscientious fashion, as is evident from the fact that hapless undergraduates would find their tutorials fixed for six o'clock in the morning. But this new example of austerity did not prevent him from being extraordinarily popular with his pupils, for whom he on his side had a very sincere regard.

After five years he was again actively engaged in parochial work, and was asked to go out to the West Indies as Archdeacon of the Barbados; but he evidently felt that his work lay in England, and he declined this offer. For some time also he felt it his duty to help his father who was now becoming old.

There was, too, a chance that he might be elected Head of his College, but this opportunity, much to his grief, he lost. It is curious that both Pusey and Newman voted against him on this occasion. Pusey lived to regret it, but Newman always felt that he had done the right thing. It is interesting to speculate what might have been the course of the Oxford Movement if Keble had become Provost of Oriel. The Head of a College was then an even more important person than he is to-day, and in the intensely oligarchic society of the university and of the nation he would have lent to the Movement a support which might have prevented the worst of the opposition, and made for gradual instead of revolutionary change.

In the same year Keble published his most famous book of poems, *The Christian Year*. He did not wish to do it and had intended to reserve publication until his death; but he yielded to the solicitations of his friends, and there were many thousands who had reason to be grateful for his decision. He himself was so diffident about the book that he could never bear to have it mentioned in his presence; but it went through edition after edition, some of them of considerable size. There were, in fact, no fewer than ninety-five editions of it during his own lifetime.

Lord David Cecil, in his anthology of Christian Poetry, deals very hardly with *The Christian Year*, and says that he can discover no poetry in it. But that only shews how far removed is our mentality to-day from that of Keble's period. The book would not have sold in such huge numbers if it had not found its way to the heart of the people and adequately met a real need. In these stirring and turbulent times there is something foreign to us in its calm and placid tone. People are apt to remember with a smile that in his preface Keble refers to the 'soothing tendency' of the Book of Common Prayer. Nowadays we do not want to be soothed by poetry, religious or secular. But if we can ever recapture that mood we shall, I think, find something really valuable in *The Christian Year*. It has a true and tender feeling for nature, a very profound religious sense, and it combines the two by making every feature of the natural world sacramental. For Keble, to quote another poet,

> Earth's crammed with heaven
> And every common bush afire with God.

But the fire is not a devouring flame. It is rather an intense glow, by contact with which one may oneself become incandescent. There are no fireworks, but the calmness of an absorbing and quiet elation.

What seems to many the turning point in Keble's history came in July 1833, when he preached his famous sermon before the Judges of Assize in the University Church. Newman always said afterwards that that was the starting point of the Oxford Movement, but it is doubtful whether anybody else felt that. Keble himself, although, of course, utterly determined and sincere in everything he said, was quite unaware that his utterance was to be in any way epoch-making. He had seized the opportunity of this State function to declaim against the recent action of the Government in amalgamating a number of the dioceses in Ireland, and he had used it as an instance of what he called the National Apostasy. To the impartial historian, looking back from the vantage point of modern times, the amalgamation seems to have been an act of belated justice; but to Keble its main significance lay in the fact that the Government had taken this action without in any way consulting the Church itself, and it was a sign of that Liberalism which was beginning to spread through every department of thought and action and appeared to denote a national apostasy from God and religion.

The Judges themselves seem not to have noticed anything untoward in the utterance, and one of them afterwards described it as 'an appropriate discourse.' But when people thought it over, it did bring to a head many of the discontents under which the most earnest and serious section of the religious public was labouring, and from that point of view it may be regarded as the

I

lever which set the vast movement of religious revival in motion.

It is well known how soon after this the Oxford friends with certain like-minded associates began to publish the *Tracts for the Times* in order to stir up the clergy and people of England to a recognition of the true implications of the Church's religion. Keble himself soon left Oxford to become Vicar of Hursley. He married, and the marriage turned out very happily. He speaks of his wife as 'his conscience, his memory and his common sense.' He found time to write eight of the *Tracts*, and also gave himself to more serious literary work. He undertook an edition of Hooker, the greatest of all writers on the Anglican Church. Keble's edition of the *Ecclesiastical Polity*, revised as it has since been, is still the standard edition of that work.

This occupation with history reveals another characteristic of Keble's mind and of the Movement with which he was associated. At that period English people had little or no sense of the past. They were satisfied with their achievements in the present, but neither in secular nor ecclesiastical affairs were they much concerned with what had happened before them. Ecclesiastically they were devoted to the idea of the Reformation, but they had only the vaguest idea of the history of that period, and from it their thought leapt straight back to the times of the Bible. The period between the Bible and the Reformation was nothing but darkness.

Keble and his friends restored a feeling for history as a whole. To them history was continuous. They did not believe that the Church of God could be found only in the Bible and in the Reformation, but they believed that it had enjoyed a continuous course from the first century to the present time. God had never left

Himself without a witness and that witness was to be found supremely in His own accredited Society. The present day was the heir of the whole past and not merely of two significant periods within it. To this view there was a corollary. It meant, of course, that the Church was an independent entity with an unbroken record. It was not dependent upon the State. It had its own rules, its own organization, its own life; and it could not be dealt with as if it were some mere department of a secular and transitory government. The Church must witness to the State of God's will and if necessary rebuke it for its failure to perform that will.

Throughout all the storm of controversy which these views excited Keble continued his work as a devoted parish priest. It seems curious that this country clergyman should have been the power on whom the two greater figures, Newman and Pusey, relied. It was from him that they drew their confidence. He was the rock on which they leaned. Keble was never conscious of any revolutionary or essential change. Whenever the others were perturbed because they were being accused of innovation, Keble's inevitable reply was, 'This is exactly what I learnt from my father.' He knew perfectly well that he was simply bringing into the light of open day a tradition which had never died out, although it had been overlaid by the complacency of both Church and State.

And it is probable that he drew a measure of his strength not only from his consciousness of tradition, but also from the fact that in his parish he lived very near to the heart of the people and saw the great system of the Church at work in the salvation of souls.

In spite of the many hours that he gave to answering correspondents from all over the country, it was to his own people that he gave his keenest devotion. He was particularly happy with the children. A new book of poems, the *Lyra Innocentium*, was written not only about children, but also for them, and it contained some of his best verses. A homely picture has been drawn of him taking his boys to play cricket on the village green on Sunday afternoon. His Confirmation classes lasted a full year, and he would walk miles in order to make up an instruction to some young person who had been obliged to miss a class.

To many it has seemed almost incredible that a person so devoted to the poor could have shewn so little interest in the great industrial revolution which in the social sphere was the strongest challenge of that period to English complacency. But it may be questioned whether Keble was more than half conscious of the hardships of the poor. It has to be remembered that he was a country clergyman, and that he had never been brought into contact with town conditions. The lot of what we nowadays call the proletariat was very different from that of a country labourer; and although it might be possible to shew on paper that the country labourer was often worse off financially, yet he lived in much closer touch with his employers, and there was still enough of the feeling of obligation on the part of landowners towards their people to ensure that they received many gifts in kind. Also the hard lot of the labourer might frequently be ameliorated through the good offices and charity of the families of the clergy and the squire.

In any case Keble was not vitally concerned with material well-being. His austerity was of such a kind that bodily comforts were to him of little importance except as an opportunity for self-denial. He belongs to that period of English religious thought when the other world was of such vast importance that in comparison with it this world was nothing. The light from heaven was so bright that it cast earth into an almost complete shadow. To him so much happiness was to be obtained in church, where he would be brought into contact with heaven, that it could atone for much dis-ease and positive misery outside. The book on Eucharistic Adoration which Keble wrote during this period is not a Party cry, but a real expression of intense worship lifting the earth-bound soul from all that would hold it down into the serene atmosphere of the courts of heaven.

Towards the close of his life the storms of controversy beat a little less furiously upon the rock that was Keble. The Scottish Church made him a Canon of Cumbrae in 1854. Newman, whose departure had been perhaps the greatest sorrow that Keble would ever have to endure, came to visit him once again at Hursley. They had been parted for twenty years, and Keble did not even recognize his guest when they met on the door-step, and Newman had to present his card. Pusey was in the house at the same time. The three old friends lunched together, and they promised to meet again; but God willed it otherwise. Mrs. Keble, whose health was never good, began to fail so much that he had to move her from one seaside place to another; and then he himself suffered a stroke and they had to return home. In the end he died first, and she rejoined him six weeks after.

I do not think that I need dwell any longer upon his character; but if I have failed to give you a sufficiently clear idea of Keble's sagacity I should like to remind you of Dr. Liddon's saying that Keble was the wisest man he had ever known. One of his modern biographers says of him that 'he possessed all the characteristics of the Saint; a man who finds his strength in the secret chamber of

spiritual communion and who goes out into the world
with a heart which radiates with the love of God and
therefore of man; who asks for no reward but to be
allowed to serve; who serves because he loves.'

That that love was returned was evidenced by the
crowd of people from all over England who attended his
funeral in the country churchyard at Hursley. As soon
as the service was over a few of the more distinguished
guests met together in the vicarage to ask what should be
done to establish a suitable memorial of one to whom the
Church owed so much. The answer was found in that
modern Oxford College which bears his name and was
designed by the same architect who built Melbourne
Cathedral. From it in the intervening century many
hundreds of students have gone out to serve God in
Church and State.

But actually the best memorial of him is to be found
in the Church itself. And I use the term Church in the
widest possible sense; for not only is there no congregation in the Anglican Communion which has not been
affected by him, but, directly or indirectly, every other
of the great denominations of Christendom has felt his
influence both in its theology and in the conduct of its
worship.

14

GRENFELL OF LABRADOR, BELOVED PHYSICIAN

IT is interesting, if not surprising, what a large percentage of the really great men of modern times have been missionaries. Three names leap at once to the mind: Gairdner of Cairo, Schweitzer of West Africa, Grenfell of Labrador. Grenfell's importance has been increased by the fact that he was granted a long life in which to mature the schemes that he initiated when still a young man.

He was seventy-six when he died, and he was not at all the ordinary person's idea of a missionary. He was one of the most 'all-round' men that European civilization has ever known. He was a sailor, surgeon, engineer, industrial leader, manufacturer, explorer, magistrate, as well as author, teacher, and preacher. In all these varied aspects his life was so bound up with those of the people to whom he ministered that his reputation will necessarily live as long as the records of that people endure.

He was a descendant of that great sea-dog, Sir Richard Grenville, around whom Tennyson wrote one of his most famous poems, and from whom no doubt he inherited some of his taste for the sea. But his own father followed the much more prosaic profession of schoolmaster; and it was actually in the surroundings of a school that he was born and spent his early years.

He was educated at Marlborough College, and from

there he went to the London Hospital to study medicine. Perhaps his greatest interest at this time was in Rugby football, and he went to Oxford just long enough to get his 'Blue.' But that was not the only form of athletics to occupy his attention. He was a great exponent of 'Fives,' and at that game he often had as his partner that well-known clerical athlete, Dr. Winnington Ingram, later Bishop of London.

Grenfell was still a very young man when he heard Dr. Moody preach in one of his Tent Missions, and realized that there was something in life beside athletics. His new-found determination to devote his energies to the cause of Christ and his fellow men was strengthened when he came in contact with J. E. K. Studd, the great Cambridge cricketer, who was also giving his life to missionary purposes.

In the direct and practical way that always characterized him Grenfell displayed his new interest by starting missionary work among the boys of the East End of London. And here he learnt a lesson that he practised throughout the rest of his active career. Finding that the boys did not want his Gospel, and that in order to prevent them breaking all his furniture he had to take them by the seat of the trousers and throw them out of the door, he determined to give them something that they did want. He turned his rooms into a gymnasium, where he convinced his London boys of his prowess with the boxing gloves. He then found himself so respected by them that at last he could preach to them the Gospel.

It was Sir Frederick Treves, King Edward VII's physician, who first directed Grenfell's attention to the work to which he was to devote the major part of his life. Treves was on the committee of the Royal National Mission to Deep Sea Fishermen, and he happened to tell Grenfell that he thought it would be worth-while seeing whether a doctor could survive the hardships of North Sea fishermen while sharing their life and ministering to them. As a result of this suggestion, in 1889, when only twenty-four years of age, Grenfell entered the service of this Mission and fitted out the first hospital ship for the North Sea Fisheries. The experience that he gained during his three years with the fishermen off the English coast stood him in good stead when he heard of the difficulties encountered by people doing similar work off the coast of Labrador, and he determined to bring his healing out to them.

In 1892 he set sail from Great Yarmouth in a ninety-seven ton steamer. Labrador has been described as 'a land of low-lying fogs and great headlands, of sudden squalls and treacherous icebergs, a land where the boats of fishermen sink under the weight of ice that forms on gunwale and oar, where men are frozen to the seats of their boats and where on angry nights the wind goes shrieking through the narrow harbours and tugs at the soft-roofed huts. When in these places the sun has sunk behind the barren hills the darkness closes down as though the hand of God had been withdrawn and Labrador has been left alone in her desolation.' The reason that lay at the heart of this new endeavour under such severe conditions can be given in his own words: 'When you set out to commend your Gospel to men who don't particularly want it, there is only one way of going about it; to do something for them that they will be sure to understand.'

His first work was done in the hospital ship, ministering to the needs of the fishermen at sea. But he soon found that the needs of those on shore were even greater. He ultimately built along the thousand miles of coast-line a series of five hospitals about two hundred miles apart, so that they should be reasonably easy of access to the sparse and scattered population. In addition, there were established seven nursing stations to act as auxiliaries to the chain of hospitals.

He found that the people of Labrador suffered not only from disease, but also from dire poverty. He tried to find some way of assisting them to eke out the money earned from their fishing. He established trading posts where they could fill in the long winter months by doing work to increase their scanty incomes. Later, finding that the traders were paying far too small a price for the fish and charging far too large a price for the living commodities they sold to the fishermen in return, he succeeded in establishing, in the face of considerable opposition, a co-operative scheme which ultimately had not only its own shops and warehouses, but even its own ships, managed by the fishermen and their families.

To some this seemed a curious occupation for a doctor, but he was convinced that the tuberculosis of which he saw so much was mostly due to undernourishment, and that the undernourishment was due to the raw deal given the fishermen by the traders. As usual his direct mind and abundant energy provided the shortest way out of the difficulty.

All this time he shared the lives of the people of Labrador to such an extent that he obtained an intimate knowledge of their hardships and of the best means of relieving them. The three months or so of summer he spent cruising in the hospital ship *Strathcona*. The long winter months he spent travelling about from post to post with his team of dogs.

He became the best known figure in that part of the world, and even attracted the attention of people at home.

Lloyds, the great insurance company, suspecting that the heavy loss of ships in those parts must be due to some malpractice, asked him to become their agent. At first he refused, thinking that it was none of his business; but presently, believing that there was some ground for their fears, he accepted. Shortly afterwards, having rescued the crew of a sunken ship, he proceeded to find the ship, managed somehow to have it examined at low tide, and found that the only thing wrong with it was that there was a big hole in the bottom obviously caused by a crowbar. A similar incident may be described in his own words:

Last season after every one had left the coast a report that a large vessel, loaded with fish and fully insured, had been lost on the rocks six hundred miles North, reached us. Owing to the rapidly forming ice we were doubtful if it were possible to get at the ship; but fortune favoured us. We were able to get her, raise her and almost to our own surprise we were able to tow her in spite of the December gales to safety. The consignee, the same man who had owned the other steamer and who had suffered other so-called 'losses,' was found guilty of barratry and sent down to penal servitude.

It is said [Dr. Grenfell continues] that the world consists of two kinds of people, those who go out and try to do something, and those who stay at home and wonder why they don't do it in some other way. How would the critics look at this? Was it missionary? Is not the real problem of Christianity how best to commend it to the world? Can it most be advocated by word or deed? Can we afford to divorce the secular from the religious any more than the religious from the secular? It seems to me that there is only one way to reach the soul, that is through the body. When the soul has cast off the body we cannot reach it at all.

There was no end to the humanitarian work that Grenfell did. He made himself responsible for efforts to raise the culture as well as the religion of the Esquimaux. Here, as so often among native peoples, one of the greatest difficulties was caused by the way in which unscrupulous white people would introduce liquor among them. This, of course, was poison to the Esquimaux. In his campaign against this evil Grenfell was helped by the fact that he had been made Magistrate, and he was able to set on foot raids against illicit saloons which were doing considerable harm not only among the natives, but among the fisher folk and their families.

The children came in for a great deal of his care. Labrador, in spite of its climate, is capable of producing very fine children, but lack of medical services, the remoteness from other children, the poverty of the parents, all made for a high percentage of disease, both mental and physical. Grenfell, with his usual energy, set himself to do what he could. In addition to his hospitals and nursing stations he set up four orphanage boarding-schools, which gave an opportunity of training in industrial as well as in purely academic subjects.

Grenfell realized that the welfare of any country must depend upon its facility of access to primary products. The barren country of Labrador appeared incapable of feeding many cattle. Such cattle as there were, and even the poultry, were in grave danger from the dogs which were bred in great numbers because of their use for transport, but which were extremely ferocious. Even human beings were not safe from them. Grenfell tells of a quite athletic young man who was killed and eaten by his own team of dogs; and of another man who set out with his wife and child in the dog-sleigh. None of the family ever returned, but the dogs did.

What was to be done? Grenfell believed that the

problem could be solved at once if reindeer were imported into the country. He found that there was a sufficient quantity of the kind of moss upon which reindeer habitually feed. The reindeer could not only supply food, but they could also supply transport, for a single reindeer is said to be capable of covering a hundred miles a day while drawing a load of 300 lbs. Grenfell tried to persuade the Government to take the matter up. Failing their help he got private assistance, collected a good deal of money in America, and actually imported three hundred reindeer from Norway. They caused great excitement when they arrived with the Lapland families in their strange costumes who had come to look after them.

In the midst of all his humanitarian work Grenfell never forgot that he was first and foremost a missionary. He preached the Gospel with a simple fervour that carried conviction more readily than any eloquence could have done. I have seen him described as 'the world's worst speaker but the most impressive.' He thought nothing of the form of oratory. The only thing that interested him was the content of the message he had to convey.

Much the same may be said of his literary activities, which were many. But here simplicity is a style of its own, and the directness of Grenfell's narrative, combined with his intense sympathy for the fishermen of whom he wrote, places his work upon a high level of artistic achievement.

Grenfell inaugurated a new era in the work of medical missions. He was one of those happy men to whom it is given even in their own lifetime to see of the travail of their soul and to be satisfied. He was a heroic and almost legendary figure long before his end came, and he retained his own buoyant and youthful spirit to the last. He was the kind of man who galvanized everything he touched. For hundreds besides himself he made life worth living. He was himself filled with the Spirit of God, and he supplied many lesser vessels from the Source at which he drew his own inspiration. Would that there were many like him.